Future-Proof Your Mainframes with AI/ML

Mainframes

Ricardo Nuqui

Published by Isaac Nangan, 2024.

FUTURE-PROOF YOUR MAINFRAMES WITH AI/ML

First edition. November 20, 2024.

ISBN: 978-9815194944

Written by Ricardo Nuqui.

Table of Contents

To Coleen, Sky and Neo. You are my inspirations.

Future-Proof Your Mainframes with AI/ML

Ricardo Nuqui

Preface

Mainframes have stood the test of time, powering some of the most critical systems in industries like finance, healthcare, and logistics. Their unmatched reliability, scalability, and efficiency have made them a cornerstone of enterprise operations for decades. Yet, the world is shifting. The rise of Artificial Intelligence (AI) and Machine Learning (ML) has opened up new possibilities for innovation, and mainframes are poised to become even more powerful as they embrace these cutting-edge technologies.

This book, **Future-Proof Your Mainframes with AI/ML**, is a response to that shift—a comprehensive guide for professionals who see the immense potential of combining the stability of mainframes with the intelligence of AI/ML. It's for those who understand that legacy systems are not relics of the past but launchpads for future innovation.

At its heart, this book is about transformation. It's about taking the systems you already know and elevating them to solve problems you've only dreamed of addressing. Whether it's automating workflows, improving predictive capabilities, or optimizing resource allocation, the integration of AI/ML into mainframe environments will help you unlock unprecedented efficiency, agility, and insights.

Throughout this book, you'll encounter a blend of theory, practical guidance, and real-world examples, carefully designed to bridge the gap between conceptual understanding and tangible implementation. Each chapter builds upon the last, ensuring that as you progress, you'll gain not only knowledge but also the confidence to apply it.

As you read, I encourage you to think about the unique challenges and opportunities within your organization. How can AI/ML help solve longstanding bottlenecks? What value can it create for your business and your customers? This book is not just a roadmap for what's possible—it's an invitation to rethink how you approach innovation in your mainframe environment.

The journey ahead is exciting and full of potential. I'm thrilled to guide you through it. Together, we'll explore how to combine the enduring power of mainframes with the dynamic possibilities of AI and ML, creating systems that are ready to thrive in the digital age.

Welcome aboard. Let's get started.

Sincerely,

Ricardo Nuqui

Prologue

Imagine a control room filled with whirring machines, blinking lights, and rows of operators monitoring systems that power the world's most vital industries. This was the mainframe's golden age—a symbol of technological sophistication, the bedrock of financial institutions, healthcare networks, and government agencies. These systems were built to last, engineered for reliability and resilience. Decades later, they remain the backbone of global enterprise operations.

But the world has changed. Today, data flows faster and in greater volumes than ever before. Customer expectations are no longer limited to "efficient service"; they demand personalized, real-time interactions. The competitive edge lies in prediction, agility, and innovation. To meet these demands, enterprises must look beyond the traditional strengths of their mainframes. They must adapt, evolve, and embrace the transformative potential of Artificial Intelligence (AI) and Machine Learning (ML).

The integration of AI/ML into mainframe environments is not a simple upgrade—it's a revolution. AI/ML allows us to predict failures before they happen, optimize workloads with unprecedented precision, and uncover patterns in data that were previously invisible. It transforms the mainframe from a stable workhorse into a smart, dynamic engine for innovation.

The journey to this future is not without its challenges. Many organizations struggle with questions like:

- How do we integrate cutting-edge AI/ML tools with

legacy mainframe systems?
- What are the risks and trade-offs of modernization?
- How do we balance the need for innovation with the security and compliance demands of our industries?

These are not theoretical concerns—they are real, pressing issues that many enterprises face today. This book was written to answer those questions and to provide a practical guide for navigating this new landscape.

But this journey is not just about technology. It's about mindset. It's about shifting from a perspective of maintaining the status quo to one of unlocking potential. It's about seeing mainframes not as relics of the past but as pillars of the future.

As you turn the pages of this book, you will discover a roadmap for transformation. You'll learn how to harness the power of AI/ML to make your mainframes more agile, intelligent, and impactful. You'll find strategies, tools, and insights designed to bridge the gap between legacy systems and next-generation technologies.

The prologue to this transformation is already being written by pioneers who see the possibilities and take the leap. By embarking on this journey, you join a growing community of innovators reshaping the role of mainframes in a digital world.

This is not just a technical challenge—it's a story of evolution and reinvention. And now, that story is yours to write.

Welcome to the future of mainframes. Let's shape it together.

Introduction

The digital age has ushered in a transformative era of technological innovation. Data-driven insights, predictive analytics, and automation are no longer optional—they are essential for enterprises to remain competitive. For decades, mainframes have been the bedrock of industries like finance, healthcare, and logistics, handling massive workloads with unmatched reliability and security. However, as the demands of modern business evolve, so too must the systems that support them.

Artificial Intelligence (AI) and Machine Learning (ML) are no longer futuristic concepts; they are tools shaping the way enterprises operate today. This book, **Future-Proof Your Mainframes with AI/ML**, is designed to guide you through the process of integrating AI/ML technologies with mainframe environments, enabling you to unlock the full potential of these powerful systems.

The Importance of AI/ML in Mainframes

Mainframes are often considered the workhorses of enterprise computing—stable, secure, and capable of processing vast amounts of data. But stability alone is no longer sufficient in an era where agility and innovation drive success.

AI and ML bring a new dimension to mainframes by enabling them to:

1. **Enhance Operational Efficiency:** AI/ML tools can automate repetitive tasks, optimize workloads, and identify inefficiencies in real time.
2. **Improve Predictive Capabilities:** With machine learning,

mainframes can predict equipment failures, customer behaviors, and market trends with high accuracy.

3. **Strengthen Security:** AI-powered anomaly detection and fraud prevention add a layer of intelligence to traditional security measures.
4. **Drive Business Insights:** By analyzing complex datasets, AI/ML can uncover patterns and trends that help enterprises make smarter decisions.

Integrating AI/ML with mainframes transforms them from reliable processing systems into dynamic platforms capable of adapting to rapidly changing business needs.

Who This Book is For

This book is for anyone who recognizes the potential of combining the strengths of mainframes with the transformative power of AI and ML. Whether you are:

- **A Mainframe Professional:** Looking to modernize legacy systems and expand your technical expertise.
- **An IT Leader or Manager:** Seeking to drive digital transformation in your organization.
- **A Data Scientist or AI Specialist:** Exploring ways to integrate AI/ML into enterprise environments.
- **A Business Executive:** Interested in understanding how AI/ML can unlock value from existing infrastructure.

No matter your role, this book provides actionable insights, practical tools, and a clear roadmap to help you achieve your goals.

How to Use This Companion Book

This book is designed to serve as both a learning resource and a practical reference:

1. **As a Guide During Your Learning Journey:**
   - Follow along with the content while taking the online course, using this book to deepen your understanding of key concepts.
   - Take advantage of additional examples, explanations, and case studies that complement the course materials.
2. **As a Practical Reference:**
   - Use this book as a hands-on resource when implementing AI/ML in your organization.
   - Refer to specific sections for guidance on data preparation, tool selection, model deployment, and optimization.

Structure of the Book

The book is divided into logical sections that build on one another, starting with foundational concepts and progressing to advanced implementation strategies. You don't need to read it cover to cover; feel free to jump to the sections most relevant to your immediate needs.

Supplementary Materials

This book also includes:

- **Checklists and Action Plans:** To help you apply the concepts in real-world scenarios.
- **Case Studies and Examples:** To illustrate successful implementations of AI/ML in mainframe environments.
- **Further Learning Opportunities:** Recommendations for

additional courses, certifications, and resources to continue your journey.

As you begin this exciting journey, remember that every step you take toward modernizing your mainframe environment is a step toward creating a smarter, more agile enterprise. The challenges are real, but so are the opportunities. With the right tools, knowledge, and mindset, you can future-proof your systems and lead your organization into the next era of innovation.

Let's get started.

Part I: Foundations of AI/ML in Mainframes

Every great transformation begins with a solid foundation, and integrating Artificial Intelligence (AI) and Machine Learning (ML) into mainframe environments is no exception. Before diving into the technical steps of modernization, it's essential to understand the principles that make AI and ML so powerful, and why they're poised to revolutionize how mainframes operate.

Mainframes have always been about stability, security, and scale—qualities that make them indispensable for critical business functions. But as industries evolve, there's a growing need for systems that can do more than process transactions or store data. Today's enterprises demand systems that can learn, adapt, and even predict the future. This is where AI and ML come into play.

AI and ML are not just buzzwords—they are the tools driving today's innovation. AI enables machines to mimic human intelligence, while ML allows systems to learn from data and improve over time. When these technologies are applied to mainframes, they unlock capabilities that were once thought to be beyond the scope of traditional systems. Imagine mainframes that:

- Automate complex decision-making processes.
- Predict equipment failures before they happen.
- Detect and prevent fraud in real time.
- Personalize customer interactions on an unprecedented scale.

To fully grasp the potential of AI/ML in mainframes, it's important to start with the basics. In this section, we'll explore the fundamental concepts behind AI and ML, breaking down what they are, how they work, and why they're so impactful. These foundational insights will serve as the building blocks for everything that follows, helping you connect the dots between the theoretical and the practical.

By understanding the core principles of AI and ML, you'll be better equipped to see the opportunities for integration within your mainframe environment. More importantly, you'll gain the confidence to lead the charge in bringing these transformative technologies into your organization.

As you progress through this part of the book, keep in mind that these are not abstract ideas—they are tools you can use to solve real-world problems. Whether you're optimizing resource allocation, enhancing customer experiences, or fortifying security, the foundations of AI and ML will provide you with the knowledge and inspiration to create systems that are not only reliable but also intelligent and adaptive.

Let's lay the groundwork for your journey into the world of AI and ML. What lies ahead is not just a shift in technology but a shift in possibilities, and it all starts here.

1. Understanding Artificial Intelligence

Artificial Intelligence (AI) is no longer the stuff of science fiction. It is a transformative technology that has seamlessly woven itself into the fabric of modern life, influencing industries and reshaping how we interact with the world. From the recommendation engines that suggest your next binge-worthy show to the predictive analytics that optimize supply chains, AI is everywhere. But what exactly is AI, and how can it elevate the capabilities of mainframe environments?

This section provides the foundation for understanding AI, delving into its core definitions and principles while showcasing its real-world impact. Whether you are new to the concept or looking to deepen your understanding, this chapter will provide clarity and context, paving the way for practical applications in your own mainframe systems.

Overview of Subtopics

Definitions and Key Concepts

At its core, AI refers to the simulation of human intelligence in machines. It enables systems to perform tasks that traditionally required human cognition, such as decision-making, problem-solving, and pattern recognition. AI spans a broad spectrum of capabilities, from rule-based systems to advanced learning models.

We will explore the following:

- **What AI Is:** A clear, concise definition of Artificial

Intelligence.

- **Types of AI:** Narrow AI (task-specific) versus General AI (human-level intelligence).
- **Core Components:** Key concepts such as natural language processing, computer vision, and reasoning.
- **The Role of Data:** Why data is the lifeblood of AI systems and how it powers intelligent behavior.

Understanding these principles is essential to see how AI can complement the unique strengths of mainframe environments, turning them into adaptive, intelligent systems.

Real-World Examples of AI in Action

AI's true power lies in its applications. Across industries, organizations are leveraging AI to tackle challenges, streamline operations, and deliver value. This subtopic will highlight examples that resonate with enterprises running mainframe systems, offering inspiration for how AI can be integrated into your own environment.

Here's what we'll cover:

- **Customer Engagement:** How AI powers personalized recommendations and chatbots.
- **Operational Efficiency:** Using AI for predictive maintenance and workload optimization.
- **Security Enhancements:** AI's role in real-time anomaly detection and fraud prevention.
- **Data Insights:** How machine learning models analyze complex datasets to uncover trends and actionable insights.

Each example will illustrate not only the capabilities of AI but also its potential to solve real-world problems, providing a clear link to the challenges faced in mainframe environments.

By the end of this chapter, you will have a clear understanding of what AI is, how it works, and the possibilities it unlocks when integrated with mainframe systems. This knowledge will set the stage for exploring the more specific discipline of Machine Learning in the next chapter and will inspire you to think about the transformative potential AI holds for your organization.

Let's begin by defining Artificial Intelligence and breaking down the key concepts that make it such a game-changing technology.

Definitions and Key Concepts

What AI Is

Artificial Intelligence (AI) can be broadly defined as the ability of machines to simulate human intelligence. It encompasses systems and algorithms capable of perceiving their environment, reasoning through available information, and taking actions to achieve specific goals. Unlike traditional programming, where a machine follows explicitly coded instructions, AI systems are designed to learn, adapt, and make decisions based on data.

In the context of mainframes, AI transforms these already powerful systems by adding an adaptive layer that enhances their capabilities. Tasks like predictive analytics, anomaly detection, and natural language interaction become not just possible but seamlessly integrated into workflows.

Types of AI

1. Narrow AI (Task-Specific AI)

Narrow AI refers to systems that are designed and trained to perform a specific task exceptionally well. Examples include:

- Chatbots that respond to customer inquiries.
- Predictive maintenance algorithms in manufacturing.
- Fraud detection systems in financial services.

Narrow AI is the most common form of AI in use today and aligns well with mainframe environments, where precision and efficiency are paramount.

2. General AI (Human-Level Intelligence)

General AI refers to systems with the ability to perform any intellectual task that a human can do. These systems would possess cognitive abilities across a wide range of domains, enabling them to reason, learn, and apply knowledge in entirely new and unforeseen ways.

- **Example:** An AI system capable of simultaneously analyzing financial data, diagnosing medical issues, and solving engineering problems.

While General AI remains largely theoretical, advancements in Narrow AI continue to lay the groundwork for broader applications.

Core Components

To understand how AI systems function, it's essential to explore their core components. These components form the foundation of how machines process and act upon data:

1. Natural Language Processing (NLP)

- Enables machines to understand, interpret, and respond to human language.
- **Applications:** Chatbots, sentiment analysis, and document processing.

Example in Mainframes: Automating customer service workflows by integrating NLP-driven chatbots that interface with legacy systems for account management.

2. Computer Vision

- The ability of machines to interpret and analyze visual data such as images or videos.

- **Applications:** Facial recognition, quality control in manufacturing, and medical imaging.

Example in Mainframes: An AI system analyzing scanned documents to extract key data fields for processing.

3. Reasoning and Decision-Making

- AI's capability to evaluate scenarios, weigh options, and make logical decisions.
- **Applications:** Automated scheduling, recommendation systems, and risk assessments.

Example in Mainframes: Optimizing resource allocation in mainframe environments during peak operational hours.

The Role of Data

Why Data is Critical to AI

AI systems rely on data to learn patterns, make predictions, and improve over time. Without high-quality, relevant data, even the most advanced AI algorithms cannot function effectively.

Key Aspects of Data in AI Systems:

1. **Training Data:** Used to teach AI models how to recognize patterns and make decisions.
2. **Validation Data:** Ensures the model performs accurately on unseen examples.
3. **Real-Time Data:** Feeds live information into AI systems for ongoing learning and adaptation.

How Mainframes Provide a Unique Advantage

Mainframes handle vast amounts of structured and unstructured data, making them ideal platforms for AI integration. Their ability to process and store data securely ensures that AI models can access the insights they need without compromising on performance or reliability.

Example:

A mainframe integrated with AI processes transaction data to detect fraudulent activity in real time, using both historical patterns and live inputs.

Conclusion

Understanding the definitions and key concepts of AI is the first step in harnessing its potential for mainframes. By exploring what AI is, its types, core components, and the central role of data, we gain the foundation to see how AI complements the unique strengths of mainframe environments. With this knowledge, you're now ready to explore real-world applications and see AI in action, bridging the gap between theoretical understanding and practical implementation.

Real-World Examples of AI in Action

The transformative potential of Artificial Intelligence (AI) comes to life through its real-world applications. By addressing specific challenges, streamlining operations, and driving value, AI has proven itself as a critical tool across industries. These examples will focus on use cases that resonate with enterprises running mainframe systems, illustrating how AI can enhance their capabilities and address common pain points.

1. Customer Engagement

AI has revolutionized the way organizations interact with their customers. By leveraging machine learning models, businesses can deliver highly personalized experiences that build loyalty and satisfaction.

Personalized Recommendations

- **How It Works:** AI algorithms analyze customer data, such as purchase history, browsing behavior, and preferences, to suggest products or services tailored to their needs.
- **Real-World Example:**
  An e-commerce company integrated AI with its mainframe system to provide real-time personalized product recommendations during online shopping sessions, boosting sales by 20%.

Chatbots for Customer Support

- **How It Works:** AI-powered chatbots use Natural

Language Processing (NLP) to understand customer queries and provide relevant responses, often accessing mainframe data for account information or transaction history.
- **Real-World Example:**
  A bank deployed an AI chatbot integrated with its mainframe to handle routine customer inquiries, such as balance checks and payment history, reducing call center workload by 30%.

---

2. Operational Efficiency

AI can optimize operations by predicting failures and automating processes, leading to cost savings and improved productivity.

Predictive Maintenance

- **How It Works:** AI models analyze data from sensors and logs to predict when equipment is likely to fail, allowing for proactive maintenance.
- **Real-World Example:**
  A manufacturing company integrated AI with its mainframe to monitor equipment performance in real time. By predicting failures before they occurred, the company reduced downtime by 40% and maintenance costs by 25%.

Workload Optimization

- **How It Works:** AI helps balance workloads across systems by analyzing demand patterns and redistributing resources dynamically.

- **Real-World Example:**
  An insurance company used AI to optimize its mainframe batch processing, reducing nightly processing time by 35%, enabling faster availability of reports for the next business day.

---

3. Security Enhancements

In a world where cyber threats are becoming more sophisticated, AI adds an intelligent layer to security systems, enabling real-time threat detection and response.

Anomaly Detection

- **How It Works:** AI models analyze patterns in network traffic, transactions, or system logs to identify unusual activities that could signal security breaches.
- **Real-World Example:**
  A financial institution integrated AI with its mainframe to monitor transactions. The system flagged a series of unauthorized transfers, preventing potential fraud worth millions of dollars.

Fraud Prevention

- **How It Works:** AI cross-references transactional data with historical patterns to identify potentially fraudulent activities.
- **Real-World Example:**
  A retail company used AI-powered fraud detection integrated with its mainframe to analyze purchase behaviors. The system identified and blocked fraudulent

credit card transactions, saving the company significant losses.

---

4. Data Insights

One of AI's most valuable capabilities is its ability to uncover patterns and insights hidden within vast datasets. This is particularly beneficial for mainframe environments, where data volume and complexity are immense.

Trend Analysis

- **How It Works:** Machine learning models sift through historical and real-time data to identify trends that can inform business decisions.
- **Real-World Example:**
  A logistics company used AI to analyze shipment data stored on its mainframe, identifying seasonal trends that helped optimize delivery routes and reduce fuel costs by 15%.

Customer Segmentation

- **How It Works:** AI clusters customers based on shared characteristics, enabling targeted marketing and personalized services.
- **Real-World Example:**
  A telecommunications provider integrated AI with its mainframe to segment customers based on usage patterns. This enabled the company to design more effective promotional campaigns, increasing customer retention by 10%.

Conclusion

These examples demonstrate the diverse and impactful ways AI can be applied to real-world challenges. From enhancing customer engagement to boosting operational efficiency, fortifying security, and unlocking valuable insights, AI offers immense potential for organizations leveraging mainframe systems.

In each of these scenarios, AI doesn't replace mainframes—it augments them, adding layers of intelligence and adaptability. As you explore AI's potential for your organization, these examples can serve as both inspiration and proof that integrating AI into mainframes is not just feasible but transformative.

Next, we'll explore **Machine Learning (ML)** in greater detail, diving into its unique characteristics and how it forms the backbone of many AI applications in mainframe environments.

2. What is Machine Learning?

Machine Learning (ML) is the engine that powers many of the most innovative applications of Artificial Intelligence (AI). While AI encompasses the broader concept of machines performing tasks that typically require human intelligence, ML focuses on enabling machines to learn from data and improve their performance over time without being explicitly programmed.

This distinction makes ML a cornerstone of modern technology, driving applications that can adapt to changing environments, recognize patterns, and make predictions with incredible accuracy. Understanding ML is essential for anyone looking to integrate AI into mainframe environments effectively.

In this section, we'll break down what ML is, how it differs from AI, and explore the algorithms and models that form its foundation.

Overview of Subtopics

How ML Differs from AI

While AI is a broad concept that includes any machine exhibiting intelligent behavior, ML is a specific subset of AI focused on learning from data. This subtopic will clarify the distinctions and explore why ML has become such a pivotal part of AI's evolution.

Key points we'll cover:

- **The AI-ML Relationship:** How ML fits within the broader AI landscape.
- **Focus on Learning from Data:** Why ML systems rely on

data to adapt and improve.

- **Examples of ML-Specific Applications:** Tasks like recommendation systems, fraud detection, and predictive maintenance, which showcase ML's unique capabilities.

Understanding this relationship will help you see how ML serves as the backbone of many AI systems, particularly in mainframe environments where large datasets are abundant.

Common Algorithms and Models in ML

At the heart of ML are the algorithms and models that allow machines to process data and make predictions. This subtopic will introduce the most commonly used approaches, explaining their mechanics and when to use them.

We'll explore:

- **Supervised Learning Algorithms:**
    - How they work: Training a model on labeled data to make predictions.
    - Examples: Linear regression, decision trees, and support vector machines (SVMs).
    - Use cases: Predicting customer churn, fraud detection, and anomaly detection in mainframes.
- **Unsupervised Learning Algorithms:**
    - How they work: Finding hidden patterns in unlabeled data.
    - Examples: K-means clustering and principal component analysis (PCA).
    - Use cases: Customer segmentation and anomaly detection in large datasets.
- **Reinforcement Learning Models:**

- How they work: Learning optimal actions through trial and error.
- Examples: Q-learning and deep Q-networks (DQNs).
- Use cases: Optimizing resource allocation and decision-making in real-time systems.

Each algorithm will be linked to practical applications in mainframe environments, providing clear examples of how ML can address real-world challenges.

Conclusion

Understanding what Machine Learning is and how it works is a critical step in leveraging its potential. By distinguishing ML from AI and exploring its most widely used algorithms, you'll gain the foundation needed to see how ML models can be applied effectively in your own systems.

In the following sections, we'll dive deeper into these subtopics, exploring the unique characteristics of ML, its practical applications, and how it can be integrated with mainframe environments to drive innovation and efficiency. Let's start by unraveling how ML stands apart from AI and why it's such a transformative technology.

How Machine Learning Differs from AI

Artificial Intelligence (AI) and Machine Learning (ML) are often used interchangeably, but they represent different aspects of intelligent systems. AI serves as the umbrella term for any technology or system capable of mimicking human intelligence. ML, on the other hand, is a specific subset of AI that enables machines to learn from data and improve over time without being explicitly programmed.

This distinction is crucial for understanding how these technologies work and where they excel. In this section, we'll explore the relationship between AI and ML, the role of data in ML, and the types of tasks where ML truly shines.

The AI-ML Relationship: How ML Fits Within the Broader AI Landscape

Artificial Intelligence encompasses a wide range of technologies and approaches aimed at creating intelligent behavior in machines. These include rule-based systems, expert systems, and, of course, Machine Learning.

- **AI's Breadth:**
  AI includes any machine-based system designed to perform tasks that typically require human intelligence, such as problem-solving, language understanding, or visual perception.
    - **Examples:** Rule-based chatbots, pathfinding algorithms in games, and robotic automation systems.
- **ML's Specific Role:**

ML focuses on creating systems that can learn and adapt by analyzing data. Rather than relying on predefined rules, ML systems identify patterns and make decisions based on past experiences.

- **Examples:** Predicting future stock prices, detecting anomalies in large datasets, or clustering customers into meaningful segments.

In essence, ML is one of the most effective tools within the AI toolkit. While traditional AI approaches can handle repetitive, rule-based tasks, ML excels in dynamic environments where data is abundant and patterns evolve over time.

Focus on Learning from Data: Why ML Systems Rely on Data to Adapt and Improve

One of the defining characteristics of ML is its reliance on data to train, adapt, and refine its models. Unlike traditional AI systems, which rely on fixed programming, ML systems improve their performance through experience.

How ML Learns from Data

1. **Training Phase:**
    - The system is fed historical data, which serves as a reference for learning patterns and relationships.
    - For example, a model predicting customer churn might analyze past customer behavior to identify at-risk users.
2. **Validation Phase:**
    - The model is tested on new data to evaluate its accuracy and reliability.
    - For example, the churn prediction model would

be tested on recent customer data to ensure it works effectively.

3. **Real-Time Adaptation:**
    - ML systems can adapt to new data inputs over time, making them suitable for dynamic environments.
    - For instance, a fraud detection system evolves as new fraud techniques emerge.

Data as the Lifeblood of ML

- **Volume and Variety:** The more diverse and abundant the data, the better the model's performance.
- **Quality Matters:** Inaccurate or incomplete data can lead to unreliable predictions or biases in the model.
- **Mainframe Relevance:** Mainframes, which handle vast amounts of structured and unstructured data, are ideal for supporting ML systems.

Examples of ML-Specific Applications

ML excels in tasks where identifying patterns, predicting outcomes, or making data-driven decisions is required. Here are some examples that showcase ML's unique capabilities:

1. Recommendation Systems

- **How It Works:**
  ML analyzes user behavior, preferences, and interactions to recommend products, services, or content.
- **Example:**
  A streaming service uses ML to recommend shows based

on viewing history.

Mainframe Application:

Retailers integrate ML-driven recommendation systems with mainframe databases to personalize shopping experiences.

2. Fraud Detection

- **How It Works:**
  ML algorithms analyze transaction patterns to flag unusual or suspicious activity.
- **Example:**
  Banks use ML to detect fraudulent credit card transactions in real time.

Mainframe Application:

Financial institutions deploy ML models on mainframes to monitor and analyze high-volume transactions for anomalies.

3. Predictive Maintenance

- **How It Works:**
  ML models analyze sensor data and historical logs to predict when equipment is likely to fail.
- **Example:**
  Manufacturers use ML to identify potential machinery failures, reducing downtime and maintenance costs.

Mainframe Application:

Organizations integrate predictive maintenance models into mainframe systems to monitor critical infrastructure, such as power grids or transportation networks.

Conclusion

While AI provides the overarching vision of intelligent systems, ML represents the most dynamic and impactful subset of AI. ML's ability to learn from data, adapt to changes, and deliver actionable insights makes it uniquely suited to solving complex, data-driven challenges in mainframe environments.

By understanding how ML differs from AI, you'll gain a deeper appreciation for its role in driving modern innovation. In the next section, we'll dive into **common algorithms and models in ML**, providing a closer look at the techniques that make it such a powerful tool for businesses and enterprises alike.

Common Algorithms and Models in Machine Learning

At the core of Machine Learning (ML) are algorithms and models that empower machines to analyze data, identify patterns, and make predictions or decisions. Choosing the right algorithm depends on the nature of the task, the type of data available, and the desired outcome. In this section, we'll explore the three main categories of ML algorithms: supervised learning, unsupervised learning, and reinforcement learning. Each will be accompanied by real-world examples, emphasizing their applications in mainframe environments.

1. Supervised Learning Algorithms

Supervised learning is one of the most widely used ML approaches, where models are trained on labeled data. This means that each input in the training dataset is paired with its corresponding correct output, allowing the model to learn the relationships between the inputs and outputs.

How They Work

- The model is fed historical data with known outcomes (labels).
- During training, it learns the mapping between inputs (features) and outputs (labels).
- Once trained, the model can make predictions on new, unseen data.

Examples of Algorithms

- **Linear Regression:** Used for predicting continuous outcomes (e.g., sales forecasting).
- **Decision Trees:** A flowchart-like structure for making decisions based on feature values.
- **Support Vector Machines (SVMs):** Separates data into categories by finding the optimal boundary.

Use Cases in Mainframe Environments

- **Predicting Customer Churn:** By analyzing historical customer behavior, a mainframe-integrated ML model can identify patterns that signal churn, enabling proactive retention strategies.
- **Fraud Detection:** Supervised models trained on labeled fraud data can detect anomalies in transactions processed by mainframes.
- **Anomaly Detection:** Decision trees or SVMs can identify irregularities in system performance or user behavior.

---

2. Unsupervised Learning Algorithms

Unsupervised learning deals with data that lacks labeled outcomes. Instead of predicting specific outputs, these models find hidden patterns or structures within the data.

How They Work

- The model processes unlabeled data and groups or organizes it based on similarities or differences.
- Common tasks include clustering and dimensionality reduction.

Examples of Algorithms

- **K-Means Clustering:** Groups data into clusters based on shared characteristics.
- **Principal Component Analysis (PCA):** Reduces the dimensionality of data while preserving its most important features.

Use Cases in Mainframe Environments

- **Customer Segmentation:** By clustering customers based on behavior or demographics, organizations can tailor marketing strategies and product offerings.
- **Anomaly Detection:** Detecting unusual patterns in large datasets processed by mainframes, such as identifying network intrusions or performance irregularities.
- **Data Exploration:** PCA can help visualize and understand large datasets stored on mainframes, simplifying complex data structures.

---

3. Reinforcement Learning Models

Reinforcement learning (RL) is a unique approach where an agent learns to take optimal actions in an environment to maximize rewards over time. Unlike supervised or unsupervised learning, RL relies on interaction and feedback.

How They Work

- The agent interacts with an environment by taking actions.
- For each action, it receives feedback in the form of rewards or penalties.

- Over time, the agent learns to choose actions that maximize cumulative rewards.

Examples of Algorithms

- **Q-Learning:** A value-based algorithm where the agent learns the quality of actions for specific states.
- **Deep Q-Networks (DQNs):** Combines deep learning with reinforcement learning for handling complex environments.

Use Cases in Mainframe Environments

- **Optimizing Resource Allocation:** RL models can learn to allocate computational resources dynamically, improving system efficiency during peak loads.
- **Decision-Making in Real-Time Systems:** For instance, in logistics, RL can optimize supply chain operations by adapting to changing demands and constraints.
- **Job Scheduling:** In mainframes, RL can help prioritize and schedule tasks to minimize processing time and maximize throughput.

Summary of Key Algorithms and Their Mainframe Applications

Algorithm/Model	Category	Mainframe Use Cases
Linear Regression	Supervised Learning	Sales forecasting, workload predictions
Decision Trees	Supervised Learning	Anomaly detection, churn prediction
Support Vector Machines	Supervised Learning	Fraud detection, system performance monitoring
K-Means Clustering	Unsupervised Learning	Customer segmentation, data exploration
Principal Component Analysis (PCA)	Unsupervised Learning	Dimensionality reduction, visualization of datasets
Q-Learning	Reinforcement Learning	Resource allocation, job scheduling
Deep Q-Networks (DQNs)	Reinforcement Learning	Real-time decision-making in logistics

Conclusion

Understanding these core algorithms and models provides a solid foundation for implementing Machine Learning in mainframe environments. Each approach, whether supervised, unsupervised, or reinforcement learning, addresses specific challenges and unlocks opportunities to optimize operations, enhance security, and deliver value.

Next, we'll delve deeper into the **Types of Machine Learning** and explore how supervised, unsupervised, and reinforcement learning fit within the broader ML landscape, along with their unique characteristics and enterprise applications.

3. Types of Machine Learning

Machine Learning (ML) is a diverse and adaptable field, with different learning paradigms designed to address a variety of problems. At its core, ML can be categorized into three main types: **supervised learning**, **unsupervised learning**, and **reinforcement learning**. Each of these types serves distinct purposes, relies on different kinds of data, and is suited for specific applications.

Understanding these types is critical for leveraging ML effectively in enterprise environments, particularly in systems that rely on mainframe computing. By recognizing the strengths and use cases of each paradigm, you can identify which approach is best suited to solve particular challenges, from improving operational efficiency to enhancing customer engagement.

Overview of Subtopics

1. Supervised, Unsupervised, and Reinforcement Learning

These three learning paradigms form the foundation of Machine Learning. Each has unique characteristics and applications:

- **Supervised Learning:**
  Models learn from labeled datasets where the outcomes are known, making it ideal for prediction and classification tasks.
    - **Examples:** Predicting customer churn, fraud detection, and demand forecasting.
- **Unsupervised Learning:**
  Models uncover hidden patterns or relationships in data

that lacks predefined labels. This approach excels at clustering and dimensionality reduction.

  - **Examples:** Customer segmentation, anomaly detection, and exploratory data analysis.

- **Reinforcement Learning:**
  An agent learns by interacting with an environment and receiving feedback in the form of rewards or penalties. This approach is ideal for dynamic, decision-making scenarios.
  - **Examples:** Resource allocation, real-time logistics optimization, and job scheduling in mainframe systems.

We'll dive deeper into how these paradigms function, their mechanics, and their differences in upcoming sections.

---

2. Use Cases in Enterprise Environments

The true value of Machine Learning lies in its practical applications, especially in enterprise settings where mainframes handle vast amounts of critical data. We'll explore how each type of ML is applied to solve real-world challenges:

- **Supervised Learning Use Cases:**
  - Automating fraud detection by analyzing transaction patterns.
  - Enhancing customer retention strategies with predictive analytics.
- **Unsupervised Learning Use Cases:**
  - Segmenting customers to improve marketing efforts and personalize services.
  - Detecting unusual patterns in network traffic to bolster security.
- **Reinforcement Learning Use Cases:**
  - Optimizing resource allocation during high-

demand periods.
  - Scheduling complex workloads to maximize efficiency in mainframe operations.

By linking these use cases to specific enterprise challenges, we'll demonstrate how ML can drive innovation and efficiency in organizations.

Conclusion

The three types of Machine Learning—supervised, unsupervised, and reinforcement learning—offer a range of tools for addressing diverse problems. By understanding the unique characteristics of each paradigm and exploring their enterprise use cases, you'll be equipped to identify and implement the most suitable ML approach for your organization.

In the following sections, we'll take a closer look at each type of learning, examining their methods, strengths, and practical applications in mainframe environments. Let's start by diving into the mechanics and applications of **supervised learning**.

Supervised, Unsupervised, and Reinforcement Learning

Machine Learning (ML) operates through three primary paradigms, each uniquely suited for solving specific types of problems. These paradigms—**Supervised Learning**, **Unsupervised Learning**, and **Reinforcement Learning**—serve as the building blocks of ML applications and enable systems to address diverse challenges across industries. Understanding their characteristics, mechanics, and use cases is essential for leveraging ML effectively, especially in enterprise environments supported by mainframes.

Supervised Learning

Supervised learning is the most common and widely applied ML paradigm. It involves training models on labeled datasets, where each input data point is paired with a corresponding output or label. The model learns to map inputs to outputs and generalize this mapping to make predictions on unseen data.

How It Works

1. **Training Phase:** The model is fed a dataset with labeled examples, such as a list of customer transactions labeled as "fraud" or "not fraud."
2. **Learning the Relationship:** The model identifies patterns and relationships between the input features and the labels.
3. **Prediction Phase:** Once trained, the model can make predictions or classifications on new, unlabeled data.

Examples of Supervised Learning Algorithms

- **Linear Regression:** Predicting continuous outcomes, such as sales or revenue.
- **Decision Trees:** Making hierarchical decisions, such as classifying loan applicants as "approved" or "denied."
- **Support Vector Machines (SVMs):** Classifying data points with complex boundaries, such as detecting fraudulent transactions.

Use Cases

- **Predicting Customer Churn:** Analyze customer behavior to predict who is likely to stop using a service, enabling proactive retention strategies.
- **Fraud Detection:** Identify suspicious transactions by learning from historical fraud patterns.
- **Demand Forecasting:** Predict future inventory or resource needs based on past trends.

Unsupervised Learning

Unsupervised learning focuses on discovering hidden patterns or structures within unlabeled data. Unlike supervised learning, there are no predefined labels or outcomes, making it ideal for exploratory data analysis and clustering tasks.

How It Works

1. **Data Exploration:** The model analyzes data to identify similarities, differences, or patterns without prior knowledge of outcomes.
2. **Pattern Recognition:** It organizes data into clusters, reduces dimensionality, or identifies anomalies.

Examples of Unsupervised Learning Algorithms

- **K-Means Clustering:** Groups data into clusters based on shared characteristics.
- **Principal Component Analysis (PCA):** Reduces the dimensionality of large datasets while preserving essential information.

Use Cases

- **Customer Segmentation:** Group customers into clusters based on behavior or demographics, enabling personalized marketing strategies.
- **Anomaly Detection:** Identify outliers in system performance, network traffic, or user behavior to enhance security.
- **Exploratory Data Analysis:** Understand the structure and characteristics of data before applying other ML models.

Reinforcement Learning

Reinforcement learning (RL) takes a completely different approach, relying on an agent that learns by interacting with an environment. The agent receives feedback in the form of rewards or penalties for its actions, and over time, it learns to maximize cumulative rewards by taking optimal actions.

How It Works

1. **Environment Interaction:** The agent observes the state of the environment and takes an action.
2. **Feedback Loop:** The agent receives feedback—a reward or

penalty—based on the outcome of its action.
3. **Policy Optimization:** Using trial and error, the agent refines its policy (the strategy for choosing actions) to achieve the best results over time.

Examples of Reinforcement Learning Algorithms

- **Q-Learning:** A value-based method where the agent learns the quality of actions for specific states.
- **Deep Q-Networks (DQNs):** Combines deep learning with RL to handle complex environments.

Use Cases

- **Resource Allocation:** Optimize the allocation of computational or physical resources during peak demand.
- **Real-Time Logistics Optimization:** Adjust supply chain operations dynamically in response to real-world constraints.
- **Job Scheduling in Mainframe Systems:** Prioritize and organize tasks to minimize processing time and maximize throughput.

Key Differences Between the Paradigms

Feature	Supervised Learning	Unsupervised Learning	Reinforcement Learning
Data Requirements	Labeled data	Unlabeled data	Interaction with an environment
Output Type	Predictive or classification outcomes	Grouping or pattern recognition	Optimal actions or policies
Training Objective	Minimize prediction error	Discover hidden patterns	Maximize cumulative rewards
Applications	Fraud detection, demand forecasting	Customer segmentation, anomaly detection	Resource allocation, real-time optimization

Conclusion

The three paradigms of Machine Learning—supervised, unsupervised, and reinforcement learning—offer a wide range of solutions for different challenges. By understanding their mechanics and applications, you'll be better equipped to choose the right approach for your specific needs.

Next, we'll explore **real-world use cases** of these paradigms in enterprise environments, demonstrating how they can address challenges such as workload optimization, security enhancement, and customer engagement in mainframe systems.

Use Cases in Enterprise Environments

The power of Machine Learning (ML) becomes evident when applied to real-world problems, particularly in enterprises where mainframes process critical workloads and massive datasets. Leveraging ML in these environments unlocks opportunities for efficiency, innovation, and strategic decision-making. This section explores practical applications of ML paradigms—**supervised learning**, **unsupervised learning**, and **reinforcement learning**—and their transformative impact on enterprise operations.

Supervised Learning Use Cases

Supervised learning excels in scenarios where outcomes are known, and historical data can be used to train models for prediction and classification tasks.

1. Automating Fraud Detection

- **The Challenge:** Enterprises process millions of transactions daily, making it impossible to manually detect fraud in real-time.
- **The Solution:** Supervised ML models analyze historical transaction data, learning to identify fraudulent patterns. Once trained, these models can flag suspicious transactions instantly.
- **Enterprise Example:**
  A financial institution integrates a supervised learning model into its mainframe. The model scans transaction data for anomalies—unusual spending patterns, atypical geolocations, or rapid-fire transactions—and triggers alerts

for further investigation.

2. Enhancing Customer Retention Strategies

- **The Challenge:** Customer churn can significantly impact revenue, but predicting which customers are likely to leave is difficult.
- **The Solution:** Supervised learning models analyze customer behavior—such as account activity, complaints, and purchase history—to predict churn risk.
- **Enterprise Example:**
  A telecommunications company uses an ML model to monitor customer interactions stored on mainframes. The system flags at-risk customers, enabling the company to send personalized offers or proactive support, increasing retention rates by 15%.

Unsupervised Learning Use Cases

Unsupervised learning is invaluable for discovering hidden patterns and structures within unlabeled datasets.

1. Segmenting Customers to Improve Marketing Efforts

- **The Challenge:** Enterprises often lack clear insights into the different types of customers they serve, leading to generalized marketing campaigns.
- **The Solution:** Unsupervised ML models, such as clustering algorithms, group customers based on shared behaviors, preferences, or demographics.
- **Enterprise Example:**
  A retail company uses a K-means clustering model to

analyze purchase histories and identify distinct customer segments, such as "frequent buyers," "bargain hunters," and "seasonal shoppers." This enables more targeted marketing campaigns and personalized promotions.

2. Detecting Unusual Patterns in Network Traffic

- **The Challenge:** Cybersecurity threats, such as unauthorized access or data breaches, are often hidden in vast amounts of network traffic.
- **The Solution:** Unsupervised ML models analyze traffic patterns to detect anomalies that deviate from normal behavior.
- **Enterprise Example:**
  An enterprise deploys an unsupervised anomaly detection model on its mainframe environment to monitor network activity. The system flags a sudden increase in outbound data transfers from a low-activity server, indicating a potential breach, allowing IT teams to respond swiftly.

Reinforcement Learning Use Cases

Reinforcement learning (RL) excels in dynamic environments where decisions need to adapt to changing conditions.

1. Optimizing Resource Allocation During High-Demand Periods

- **The Challenge:** Mainframes often face peak loads during specific times, requiring dynamic resource allocation to maintain performance.
- **The Solution:** RL models learn optimal resource

allocation strategies by trial and error, adjusting resources in real-time based on demand.

- **Enterprise Example:**
  A banking institution uses RL to allocate computing resources for peak transaction volumes during holidays. The system ensures critical processes receive priority, maintaining performance without over-provisioning resources.

2. Scheduling Complex Workloads

- **The Challenge:** Mainframes manage thousands of jobs daily, requiring efficient scheduling to minimize processing time and maximize throughput.
- **The Solution:** RL models optimize scheduling by learning from historical job execution data and adjusting task priorities dynamically.
- **Enterprise Example:**
  An insurance company uses an RL-based scheduler to manage overnight batch jobs. By prioritizing high-value tasks and minimizing idle processing time, the system reduces nightly batch processing time by 20%.

Key Takeaways

Supervised Learning in Action

- Enables real-time decision-making in fraud detection and predictive analytics.
- Relies on labeled datasets to identify trends and forecast outcomes.

Unsupervised Learning in Action

- Reveals hidden insights through clustering and anomaly detection.
- Addresses challenges in segmentation and exploratory data analysis.

Reinforcement Learning in Action

- Excels in dynamic, decision-heavy scenarios like resource allocation and job scheduling.
- Adapts to real-time changes, improving operational efficiency and reducing costs.

Conclusion

Each ML paradigm—supervised, unsupervised, and reinforcement learning—offers unique capabilities that address specific enterprise challenges. By aligning these paradigms with the needs of mainframe environments, organizations can unlock efficiencies, enhance security, and deliver personalized experiences to their customers.

In the next section, we'll explore **how to prepare your mainframe environment** for AI/ML integration, ensuring it is ready to handle the demands of modern machine learning applications.

4. The AI/ML Workflow

The successful implementation of Artificial Intelligence (AI) and Machine Learning (ML) in any environment, including mainframes, relies on a well-defined workflow. This workflow encompasses the key stages of building, testing, and deploying models, each of which is essential for creating robust and effective AI/ML systems. By understanding and mastering this process, organizations can ensure that their AI/ML initiatives deliver meaningful and actionable results.

In this section, we will break down the AI/ML workflow into its core components, exploring the intricacies of training, testing, and deploying models. Additionally, we'll address the common challenges that arise at each stage and provide strategies to overcome them, ensuring a smoother path to integration and implementation.

Overview of Subtopics

1. Training, Testing, and Deploying Models

The journey of an AI/ML model begins with training, where it learns from historical data, and progresses to testing and deployment, where it proves its effectiveness and delivers value in real-world applications.

We will explore:

- **Training Models:**
    - Feeding data to the model and enabling it to recognize patterns and relationships.
    - Choosing the right algorithms and

hyperparameters to maximize performance.

- **Testing Models:**
    - Evaluating the model's accuracy, reliability, and robustness using unseen data.
    - Identifying and addressing potential issues such as overfitting or underfitting.
- **Deploying Models:**
    - Integrating trained models into mainframe environments or enterprise systems.
    - Ensuring scalability and real-time operation for production-level applications.

These stages form the foundation of AI/ML projects and are critical for achieving long-term success.

---

2. Common Challenges and How to Overcome Them

The AI/ML workflow is not without its challenges. From data quality issues to deployment hurdles, organizations often face obstacles that can delay or derail their initiatives.

We will discuss:

- **Data Challenges:**
    - Incomplete, biased, or low-quality data affecting model performance.
    - Strategies for cleaning, preprocessing, and augmenting datasets.
- **Model Training Issues:**
    - Balancing complexity and accuracy to avoid overfitting or underfitting.
    - Tuning hyperparameters and selecting appropriate algorithms.

- **Deployment Hurdles:**
    - Integrating models with legacy systems or mainframes.
    - Ensuring scalability, real-time operation, and minimal downtime during deployment.

Understanding these challenges and their solutions will empower organizations to navigate the AI/ML workflow with greater confidence and efficiency.

Conclusion

Mastering the AI/ML workflow is a crucial step in turning concepts into actionable solutions. By delving into the training, testing, and deployment phases, as well as addressing common challenges, this section will equip you with the knowledge and strategies needed to build and maintain successful AI/ML systems.

In the next sections, we'll start by examining the **training phase**, where models learn from data to form the basis of their predictive and analytical capabilities. From there, we'll guide you through the testing and deployment stages, culminating in a complete understanding of the AI/ML lifecycle. Let's begin this transformative journey.

Training, Testing, and Deploying Models

The lifecycle of an AI/ML model revolves around three key stages: **training**, **testing**, and **deployment**. These stages are interconnected, each building upon the last to create robust, reliable, and effective machine learning solutions. Whether working with traditional systems or modern mainframes, mastering these phases is critical for achieving meaningful results. This section explores each stage in detail, highlighting their processes, challenges, and best practices.

1. Training Models

Training is the foundational phase where an AI/ML model learns from historical data. The goal is to enable the model to identify patterns, relationships, and insights that can be used to make predictions or decisions.

How It Works

- **Feeding Data:**
    - A training dataset containing input features and their corresponding labels (for supervised learning) or raw inputs (for unsupervised learning) is used to teach the model.
    - Example: A supervised learning model might analyze customer transaction data labeled as "fraud" or "not fraud" to learn patterns indicative of fraudulent behavior.
- **Pattern Recognition:**

  - The model uses algorithms to find mathematical relationships within the data, such as trends, clusters, or correlations.
  - Example: A regression model might identify how product pricing affects sales volumes.

Key Steps

1. **Selecting the Algorithm:** Choose an algorithm appropriate for the task (e.g., regression, classification, clustering).
2. **Tuning Hyperparameters:** Adjust settings like learning rate or tree depth to optimize model performance.
3. **Iterative Refinement:** Continuously refine the model as it learns from the training data.

Best Practices

- Use a diverse and representative training dataset to ensure the model learns accurately.
- Monitor for **overfitting**, where the model memorizes the training data instead of generalizing from it.

---

2. Testing Models

Once trained, the model must be evaluated to determine its accuracy, reliability, and robustness. Testing ensures that the model performs well on new, unseen data.

How It Works

- **Validation:** The model is tested on a validation dataset—a subset of the original data not used during training.

- **Performance Metrics:** Metrics like accuracy, precision, recall, and F1 score are calculated to gauge model effectiveness.

Key Steps

1. **Using a Test Dataset:** Assess how well the model performs on real-world scenarios.
    - Example: A churn prediction model is tested on customer data from the last quarter to validate its predictions.
2. **Identifying Issues:** Evaluate for common problems such as:
    - **Overfitting:** When the model performs well on training data but poorly on new data.
    - **Underfitting:** When the model fails to capture important patterns in the data.

Best Practices

- Split your dataset into training, validation, and test subsets to ensure unbiased evaluation.
- Use cross-validation techniques to maximize model robustness.
- Analyze error cases to understand where the model struggles and refine it accordingly.

---

3. Deploying Models

Deployment is the final phase, where the trained and tested model is integrated into a production environment. The goal is to enable real-time or batch processing, ensuring the model delivers actionable insights or predictions to end-users.

How It Works

- **Integration with Systems:** The model is connected to enterprise systems, such as mainframes, via APIs or middleware.
  - Example: A fraud detection model deployed on a mainframe flags suspicious transactions during payment processing.
- **Real-Time Operation:** For tasks like anomaly detection, the model processes live data streams and generates instant alerts.

Key Steps

1. **Scalability:** Ensure the model can handle large datasets or high transaction volumes without performance degradation.
2. **Monitoring:** Continuously monitor the model's predictions to identify drift or accuracy issues over time.
3. **Maintenance:** Periodically retrain the model with new data to keep it up-to-date with evolving trends.

Best Practices

- Design deployment pipelines that allow for seamless updates and scalability.
- Set up monitoring tools to track model performance in production.
- Collaborate with IT teams to ensure compatibility with legacy systems or mainframes.

Conclusion

Training, testing, and deploying models form the foundation of any successful AI/ML project. Each phase requires meticulous attention to detail and a clear understanding of both the model's mechanics and the operational environment.

- **Training** ensures the model learns meaningful patterns from data.
- **Testing** validates the model's ability to generalize and perform in real-world scenarios.
- **Deployment** brings the model into production, where it delivers actionable insights and measurable value.

By mastering these stages, organizations can build AI/ML systems that are accurate, scalable, and impactful. In the next section, we'll explore **common challenges** that arise during these phases and provide practical strategies for overcoming them, ensuring your AI/ML initiatives achieve long-term success.

Common Challenges and How to Overcome Them

The AI/ML workflow, while transformative, is not without its challenges. Organizations often encounter obstacles that, if left unresolved, can undermine the success of their AI/ML initiatives. These challenges span across the data preparation, model training, and deployment stages. Understanding these hurdles and implementing effective solutions is essential for building robust, scalable, and impactful AI/ML systems.

1. Data Challenges

The Challenge: Incomplete, Biased, or Low-Quality Data

AI/ML systems are only as good as the data they are trained on. Data issues are among the most common barriers to effective model performance.

- **Incomplete Data:** Missing values or records can result in a model that fails to generalize or makes inaccurate predictions.
- **Biased Data:** Data that reflects historical inequities or imbalances can lead to biased outcomes.
- **Low-Quality Data:** Errors, inconsistencies, or irrelevant features can distort model learning.

Solutions: Cleaning, Preprocessing, and Augmenting Datasets

1. **Data Cleaning:**
    - Identify and fill in missing values using techniques

    like mean imputation or predictive modeling.
    - Remove duplicate or irrelevant records to improve data quality.
2. **Bias Mitigation:**
    - Use representative datasets that cover diverse populations or scenarios.
    - Apply techniques such as re-sampling, re-weighting, or adversarial de-biasing.
3. **Data Augmentation:**
    - Enhance datasets by generating synthetic data that mimics real-world variations.
    - Example: In image processing, techniques like flipping, rotation, or color adjustments are used to expand datasets.
4. **Preprocessing:**
    - Normalize and standardize features to ensure consistent scales.
    - Apply dimensionality reduction (e.g., PCA) to remove irrelevant features while preserving meaningful information.

---

2. Model Training Issues

The Challenge: Balancing Complexity and Accuracy

Training a model involves striking a delicate balance between simplicity and complexity.

- **Overfitting:** A model that performs exceptionally well on training data but poorly on new data due to excessive complexity.
- **Underfitting:** A model that fails to capture important

patterns, leading to poor performance on both training and test data.

Solutions: Tuning Hyperparameters and Selecting Algorithms

1. **Regularization Techniques:**
    - Use methods like L1 or L2 regularization to prevent overfitting by penalizing overly complex models.
2. **Cross-Validation:**
    - Split data into multiple subsets to evaluate the model's performance across different samples, ensuring it generalizes well.
3. **Hyperparameter Tuning:**
    - Optimize parameters such as learning rate, depth of decision trees, or number of layers in a neural network.
    - Tools like Grid Search or Bayesian Optimization can automate this process.
4. **Algorithm Selection:**
    - Choose algorithms that align with the complexity and size of the data.
    - For example:
        - Linear regression for simple, interpretable relationships.
        - Neural networks for highly complex datasets with non-linear patterns.

---

3. Deployment Hurdles

The Challenge: Integrating Models with Legacy Systems or Mainframes

Deploying AI/ML models into existing enterprise environments, especially mainframes, introduces unique challenges:

- **Compatibility Issues:** Legacy systems may lack APIs or middleware to support modern AI/ML frameworks.
- **Operational Downtime:** Transitioning to a new system may disrupt business operations.

The Challenge: Ensuring Scalability and Real-Time Operation

- **Scalability:** AI/ML systems must handle growing data volumes and increasing workloads without degradation.
- **Real-Time Operation:** For applications like fraud detection, predictions must be generated instantaneously.

Solutions: Streamlining Deployment

1. **Integration with Mainframes:**
    - Use middleware or APIs to connect models with mainframe systems seamlessly.
    - Example: IBM z/OS Connect enables integration of mainframe data with AI platforms like IBM Watson.
2. **Containerization and Microservices:**
    - Deploy models in containers (e.g., Docker) to ensure portability and scalability across systems.
    - Use microservices architectures to isolate AI/ML functions, making them easier to scale and maintain.
3. **Monitoring and Maintenance:**
    - Implement real-time monitoring tools to track model performance and detect drift in accuracy or predictions.

   - Set up automated retraining pipelines to keep the model updated with the latest data.
4. **Minimizing Downtime:**
   - Use blue-green deployment strategies to switch between current and new versions of the model with minimal disruption.
   - Test deployments in staging environments before rolling them out to production.

Key Takeaways

Challenge	Solution
Incomplete, biased, or low-quality data	Clean, preprocess, augment, and mitigate bias in datasets.
Overfitting or underfitting	Use regularization, cross-validation, and hyperparameter tuning to balance complexity and accuracy.
Integration with legacy systems	Leverage middleware, APIs, containerization, and microservices for seamless deployment.
Scalability and real-time operation	Design scalable architectures, implement monitoring tools, and automate retraining pipelines.

Conclusion

Overcoming the challenges of data quality, model training, and deployment is vital for the success of AI/ML projects. By addressing these hurdles with proactive strategies, organizations can unlock the full potential of AI/ML in enterprise environments.

Part II: Exploring the Role of AI/ML in Mainframes

Mainframes have long been the backbone of enterprise systems, processing massive amounts of critical data with unmatched reliability and scalability. With the advent of Artificial Intelligence (AI) and Machine Learning (ML), these legacy systems are undergoing a transformation, evolving into intelligent platforms that can analyze, adapt, and drive decisions in real time. The integration of AI/ML into mainframe environments represents not just a technological enhancement but a strategic leap toward unlocking new levels of efficiency, innovation, and competitive advantage.

In this part, we delve into how AI/ML intersects with mainframes to address contemporary business challenges. From enhancing operational processes to driving customer engagement and uncovering actionable insights, we will explore the transformative impact of these technologies. By examining real-world applications, use cases, and business benefits, you will gain a deeper understanding of the unique opportunities AI/ML brings to mainframe environments.

Whether you are looking to optimize workloads, detect fraud in real time, or gain a competitive edge through predictive analytics, this part will provide the insights needed to see how AI/ML can revolutionize your organization's use of mainframes.

Let's explore the remarkable synergy between AI/ML and mainframes and uncover how these powerful tools are shaping the future of enterprise computing.

5. AI/ML Applications in Enterprise Systems

The integration of Artificial Intelligence (AI) and Machine Learning (ML) into enterprise systems is revolutionizing the way businesses operate. By enabling systems to analyze data, predict trends, and automate processes, AI/ML technologies are driving efficiency and fostering innovation across industries. For organizations running mainframes, this transformation represents a unique opportunity to modernize legacy systems and unlock their full potential in today's data-driven world.

In this section, we'll explore the broad applications of AI/ML in enterprise environments, focusing on how these technologies enhance operational efficiency and spark innovation. Additionally, we'll examine real-world examples of AI/ML implementations in industries that rely heavily on mainframe systems, demonstrating the tangible impact of these advanced technologies.

Overview of Subtopics

1. Driving Efficiency and Innovation

AI/ML technologies streamline operations by automating repetitive tasks, identifying inefficiencies, and enabling data-driven decision-making. This subtopic will cover how organizations can:

- **Optimize Resources:** Use predictive analytics to allocate resources more effectively.
- **Automate Processes:** Implement AI-powered systems to reduce manual workloads and improve accuracy.

- **Enhance Decision-Making:** Leverage ML models to generate insights and identify opportunities for growth.

We'll delve into specific scenarios, such as workload optimization, real-time anomaly detection, and predictive maintenance, showing how AI/ML can transform core enterprise functions.

2. Industry Examples of AI/ML on Mainframes

AI/ML is already delivering significant value in industries that depend on mainframes for their operations. This subtopic will explore real-world examples, including:

- **Financial Services:** Fraud detection, credit scoring, and risk analysis powered by AI/ML models integrated with mainframe systems.
- **Retail:** Personalization engines that analyze customer behavior and recommend products or promotions.
- **Healthcare:** Predictive analytics for patient care, resource allocation, and operational efficiency in hospital systems.

By showcasing these examples, we'll highlight the versatility and impact of AI/ML in enterprise environments, offering inspiration for potential applications in your organization.

Conclusion

The applications of AI/ML in enterprise systems are vast and transformative, offering solutions to long-standing challenges and opening new avenues for innovation. By exploring how these technologies drive efficiency and foster innovation, as well as examining real-world industry examples, this section will provide a comprehensive understanding of AI/ML's role in reshaping enterprise operations.

In the next section, we'll dive into the details of how AI/ML technologies enhance efficiency, automate processes, and deliver actionable insights to organizations running mainframes. Let's begin by exploring how these technologies drive operational excellence and fuel innovation.

Driving Efficiency and Innovation

AI and ML technologies have become pivotal tools for streamlining enterprise operations and fostering innovation. By automating repetitive tasks, identifying inefficiencies, and empowering data-driven decision-making, these technologies enable organizations to achieve higher productivity and uncover new growth opportunities. For enterprises reliant on mainframes, integrating AI/ML can revolutionize resource management, process automation, and decision-making capabilities.

1. Optimize Resources

Effective resource allocation is a cornerstone of operational efficiency, particularly in enterprises managing large-scale systems like mainframes. AI/ML technologies use predictive analytics to anticipate demand, identify resource bottlenecks, and optimize allocation.

How It Works

- **Predictive Analytics:** AI/ML models analyze historical data to forecast future needs, enabling proactive resource management.
- **Dynamic Allocation:** Machine learning algorithms adjust resource distribution in real time, ensuring high-priority tasks receive adequate support.

Example Use Cases

- **Workload Optimization:** In mainframes, AI-powered

systems monitor system workloads and dynamically allocate computing resources to prevent overloading and ensure consistent performance.
- **Capacity Planning:** Enterprises use ML to predict peak usage periods, helping them allocate storage, processing power, and network bandwidth efficiently.

Impact: Optimizing resources reduces operational costs, minimizes system downtime, and ensures smooth operations even during peak demand periods.

---

2. Automate Processes

Manual processes, while reliable in some cases, often lead to inefficiencies, errors, and delays. AI-powered systems can automate these repetitive tasks, improving accuracy and freeing up human resources for higher-value activities.

How It Works

- **Task Automation:** AI systems learn workflows and execute tasks such as data entry, report generation, or transaction validation without human intervention.
- **Intelligent Process Automation (IPA):** Combines ML and robotic process automation (RPA) to create smart systems capable of adapting to changing scenarios.

Example Use Cases

- **Real-Time Anomaly Detection:** AI systems automatically flag unusual activity, such as security breaches or system malfunctions, reducing response times.
- **Automated Compliance Checks:** In industries like

finance, AI/ML models review transactions to ensure they adhere to regulatory standards.

Impact: Automating processes reduces error rates, accelerates task completion, and allows employees to focus on strategic initiatives.

3. Enhance Decision-Making

AI/ML technologies empower organizations to make better decisions by uncovering actionable insights from vast amounts of data. These insights enable leaders to identify opportunities for growth, address potential risks, and adapt to market changes.

How It Works

- **Advanced Analytics:** ML models process structured and unstructured data to identify trends, patterns, and correlations that would be difficult to detect manually.
- **Predictive Modeling:** AI systems simulate scenarios to evaluate the potential outcomes of different decisions.

Example Use Cases

- **Predictive Maintenance:** In mainframe environments, ML models analyze system logs and sensor data to predict when hardware or software components might fail, allowing for preemptive action.
- **Customer Insights:** AI systems analyze customer behavior, identifying preferences and trends that inform marketing strategies or product development.

Impact: Enhancing decision-making leads to faster, more informed choices, enabling organizations to stay competitive and proactive.

Specific Scenarios in AI/ML Integration

1. Workload Optimization

AI/ML algorithms monitor and manage workloads on mainframes, ensuring efficient distribution of tasks and maintaining system stability.

- Example: A retail enterprise uses ML to optimize payment processing during Black Friday, preventing slowdowns during high transaction volumes.

2. Real-Time Anomaly Detection

AI models analyze real-time data streams to detect unusual patterns, such as a sudden spike in network activity or irregular transaction behavior.

- Example: A bank integrates AI into its mainframe to detect fraudulent transactions within seconds, minimizing potential losses.

3. Predictive Maintenance

ML models identify signs of wear and tear in hardware or software systems, allowing for repairs before failures occur.

- Example: A transportation company uses predictive maintenance to keep its mainframe-powered scheduling systems operational, avoiding costly delays.

Conclusion

AI/ML technologies are powerful enablers of efficiency and innovation, transforming enterprise operations through resource optimization, process automation, and enhanced decision-making. By implementing AI/ML in areas such as workload optimization, anomaly detection, and predictive maintenance, organizations can achieve greater agility, cost savings, and strategic insight.

In the next section, we'll explore **real-world industry examples of AI/ML in action**, showcasing how these technologies are driving transformation in sectors such as finance, retail, and healthcare.

Industry Examples of AI/ML on Mainframes

AI/ML technologies are transforming industries that rely heavily on mainframes, enabling organizations to tackle complex challenges, optimize processes, and deliver value more effectively. These examples from financial services, retail, and healthcare highlight the versatility and impact of AI/ML integration into mainframe environments, showcasing how enterprises can leverage these technologies to drive innovation and efficiency.

1. Financial Services

Mainframes are the backbone of the financial services industry, processing vast amounts of transactional and customer data with high reliability. AI/ML integration has elevated their role, enabling real-time insights and predictive capabilities.

Applications

1. **Fraud Detection**
    - **Challenge:** Detecting fraudulent activities in high-volume transaction streams is a critical yet complex task.
    - **Solution:** AI/ML models analyze transaction patterns and flag anomalies, such as unusual purchasing behaviors or rapid transfers across accounts.
    - **Example:** A global bank integrates ML-powered fraud detection models into its mainframe system, identifying suspicious activity within milliseconds

and reducing financial losses by 30%.

2. **Credit Scoring**
    - **Challenge:** Assessing creditworthiness requires analyzing diverse datasets, from income histories to spending habits.
    - **Solution:** AI models evaluate customer data and assign credit scores based on risk factors, enabling faster and more accurate loan approvals.
    - **Example:** A financial institution uses ML algorithms to process credit applications in real time, reducing decision-making times from days to minutes.
3. **Risk Analysis**
    - **Challenge:** Financial risks, such as market volatility and regulatory compliance, require sophisticated modeling.
    - **Solution:** AI-powered systems predict market trends and assess risks, helping institutions make informed investment decisions.
    - **Example:** An investment firm employs AI models on its mainframe to simulate various market conditions, optimizing portfolio strategies for risk mitigation.

---

2. Retail

Retailers increasingly rely on mainframes to manage inventory, supply chains, and customer interactions. AI/ML integration has allowed these systems to go beyond transactional processing, enabling personalized customer experiences and operational efficiencies.

Applications

1. **Personalization Engines**
    - **Challenge:** Delivering tailored recommendations to customers at scale requires analyzing vast datasets.
    - **Solution:** AI-powered personalization engines use machine learning models to analyze purchase histories, browsing behaviors, and preferences.
    - **Example:** A leading e-commerce retailer integrates ML models with its mainframe, generating product recommendations that increase conversion rates by 20%.
2. **Demand Forecasting**
    - **Challenge:** Predicting inventory needs is critical to avoid overstocking or shortages.
    - **Solution:** AI models analyze sales trends, seasonal patterns, and external factors such as weather to forecast demand accurately.
    - **Example:** A supermarket chain uses AI models on its mainframe to predict product demand, reducing inventory costs by 15% while improving availability.
3. **Customer Segmentation**
    - **Challenge:** Identifying distinct customer groups for targeted marketing requires deep data analysis.
    - **Solution:** Unsupervised ML algorithms segment customers based on purchasing habits and demographics, enabling personalized marketing campaigns.
    - **Example:** A retail giant clusters its customer base

into categories like "frequent shoppers" and "bargain hunters," tailoring promotions to each segment and boosting engagement.

---

3. Healthcare

In healthcare, mainframes play a critical role in managing patient records, insurance claims, and operational logistics. AI/ML integration has expanded their capabilities, enabling predictive analytics and real-time decision-making.

Applications

1. **Predictive Analytics for Patient Care**
   - **Challenge:** Identifying at-risk patients and predicting health outcomes is essential for proactive care.
   - **Solution:** AI models analyze patient data to predict complications, enabling early intervention.
   - **Example:** A hospital integrates predictive models into its mainframe, identifying patients at risk of readmission and implementing targeted care plans, reducing readmission rates by 18%.
2. **Resource Allocation**
   - **Challenge:** Efficiently allocating resources such as beds, staff, and equipment is crucial for operational efficiency.
   - **Solution:** ML models analyze historical and real-time data to optimize resource distribution.
   - **Example:** A healthcare provider uses AI on its mainframe to predict bed occupancy and

schedule staff accordingly, improving patient care and reducing wait times.

3. **Operational Efficiency**
    - **Challenge:** Streamlining administrative processes like billing and claims management is time-intensive and prone to errors.
    - **Solution:** AI models automate claims processing and billing verification, reducing manual workloads.
    - **Example:** An insurance company integrates ML models into its mainframe, reducing claim processing times by 40% while improving accuracy.

Key Takeaways

Cross-Industry Benefits of AI/ML on Mainframes

Industry	Application	Impact
Financial Services	Fraud detection, credit scoring	Reduced losses, faster decision-making
Retail	Personalization engines, demand forecasting	Improved customer engagement, lower costs
Healthcare	Predictive patient care, resource allocation	Enhanced care quality, operational efficiency

Why Mainframes and AI/ML Are a Perfect Match

- **Reliability:** Mainframes handle mission-critical data with high reliability, making them ideal for supporting AI/ML models that require stable environments.
- **Scale:** Mainframes process vast amounts of data, providing

the necessary volume for training and deploying AI/ML models.

- **Integration:** AI/ML enhances existing mainframe capabilities, extending their value while modernizing enterprise systems.

Conclusion

From financial services to retail and healthcare, AI/ML integration on mainframes is delivering measurable value, transforming operations, and driving innovation. These real-world examples demonstrate the versatility and potential of AI/ML to revolutionize industries.

In the next section, we'll explore **the business benefits of AI/ML integration**, examining how these technologies drive cost savings, enhance reliability, and provide a competitive advantage.

6. AI/ML Use Cases for Mainframes

Mainframes have long been the cornerstone of enterprise systems, managing high-volume transactions and mission-critical workloads with unparalleled reliability. The integration of Artificial Intelligence (AI) and Machine Learning (ML) has opened new avenues for utilizing these powerful systems, allowing enterprises to address complex challenges with greater efficiency and precision.

This section focuses on specific AI/ML use cases for mainframes, highlighting how these technologies enhance system performance, resource utilization, and security. By leveraging AI/ML, mainframes can evolve from static processing units into dynamic, adaptive systems that meet the demands of modern enterprises.

Overview of Subtopics

1. Predictive Maintenance and Anomaly Detection

Mainframes are critical to enterprise operations, and unplanned downtime can result in significant financial and operational losses. AI/ML technologies enable predictive maintenance and anomaly detection by identifying early signs of potential issues.

- **Predictive Maintenance:** Analyze historical performance data to forecast hardware or software failures before they occur, allowing for preemptive action.
- **Anomaly Detection:** Use ML models to identify unusual patterns in system logs, resource usage, or transaction data, flagging potential problems in real-time.

2. Workload Optimization and Resource Allocation

Mainframes handle diverse and often unpredictable workloads. AI/ML can optimize these processes to improve efficiency and reduce costs.

- **Workload Optimization:** Balance system loads dynamically by analyzing workload patterns and reallocating resources to prevent bottlenecks.
- **Resource Allocation:** Ensure that critical applications receive priority access to resources, improving overall system performance during peak periods.

3. Enhancing Security and Fraud Detection

The high-value data stored on mainframes makes them a target for cyber threats and fraud. AI/ML models enhance security by detecting potential risks in real-time and responding proactively.

- **Security:** Monitor network traffic and user activity to identify unusual behaviors or potential breaches.
- **Fraud Detection:** Analyze transaction data to detect fraudulent activities such as unauthorized access or suspicious financial transactions.

Conclusion

The use cases for AI/ML on mainframes demonstrate the transformative potential of these technologies. From preventing system failures and optimizing workloads to enhancing security, AI/

ML provides actionable insights and capabilities that elevate the value of mainframe systems.

In the next section, we'll dive deeper into each of these use cases, starting with **Predictive Maintenance and Anomaly Detection**, exploring how AI/ML can prevent costly downtime and ensure uninterrupted operations.

Predictive Maintenance and Anomaly Detection

Mainframes play a vital role in the daily operations of enterprises, handling high-stakes workloads and processing mission-critical data. Any unplanned downtime in these systems can result in severe financial losses, disruptions to business operations, and reputational damage. AI/ML technologies offer proactive solutions by enabling **predictive maintenance** and **anomaly detection**, transforming the way organizations manage and maintain their mainframe systems.

1. Predictive Maintenance

Predictive maintenance is a proactive approach to system management that uses AI/ML models to anticipate potential failures before they happen. This method reduces unplanned downtime, minimizes repair costs, and enhances overall system reliability.

How It Works

1. **Data Collection:**
    - Historical data from system logs, sensor outputs, and performance metrics are gathered and analyzed.
    - Examples of data points include CPU usage, memory allocation, disk I/O, and error logs.
2. **Model Training:**
    - Machine learning models are trained to identify patterns or trends that precede system failures.
    - Example: A model might detect that increasing

CPU temperatures often correlate with upcoming hardware malfunctions.

3. **Forecasting Failures:**
    - The trained model predicts when components are likely to fail, enabling preemptive action, such as scheduling maintenance or replacing parts.

Benefits of Predictive Maintenance

- **Reduced Downtime:** Maintenance can be scheduled at convenient times, avoiding unexpected disruptions.
- **Cost Savings:** Early intervention prevents minor issues from escalating into costly repairs or replacements.
- **Increased System Reliability:** Proactive maintenance ensures the system remains operational at peak efficiency.

Use Case Example

A financial services company uses predictive maintenance on its mainframe to monitor hard disk performance. The ML model identifies unusual increases in disk write errors, prompting the IT team to replace the affected drives before they fail, preventing transaction delays and ensuring uninterrupted service.

---

2. Anomaly Detection

Anomaly detection focuses on identifying irregular or unexpected patterns in system behavior. These anomalies often signal potential issues, such as security breaches, system inefficiencies, or hardware failures.

How It Works

1. **Baseline Behavior Analysis:**

    - AI/ML models are trained on historical data to understand normal system behavior, such as expected resource usage, transaction volumes, or network activity.
2. **Real-Time Monitoring:**
    - Once deployed, the model continuously monitors system metrics, comparing live data against the baseline.
3. **Flagging Anomalies:**
    - Any deviation from normal behavior—such as sudden spikes in CPU usage or unusual access patterns—is flagged for further investigation.

Benefits of Anomaly Detection

- **Early Problem Identification:** Issues are identified before they escalate, allowing for timely intervention.
- **Enhanced Security:** Suspicious activities, such as unauthorized access or data exfiltration, are detected in real-time.
- **Operational Efficiency:** Continuous monitoring ensures that inefficiencies are addressed promptly, maintaining optimal performance.

Use Case Example

A retail company uses anomaly detection to monitor its mainframe's transaction data. When the model identifies an unusual surge in failed payment attempts, it triggers an alert. The IT team discovers a configuration error in the payment gateway and resolves the issue before it impacts customers.

Key Differences Between Predictive Maintenance and Anomaly Detection

Aspect	Predictive Maintenance	Anomaly Detection
Focus	Anticipating potential failures	Identifying unusual or unexpected system behavior
Output	Forecast of when failures might occur	Real-time alerts for deviations from normal behavior
Data Requirements	Historical performance data	Baseline data for normal behavior
Examples	Forecasting hardware failure	Detecting sudden spikes in transaction failures

Integration of Predictive Maintenance and Anomaly Detection

Combining these two approaches provides a comprehensive system monitoring strategy:

- **Predictive Maintenance** ensures components are maintained proactively to prevent failures.
- **Anomaly Detection** monitors live activity, identifying deviations that could signal immediate issues.

Conclusion

AI/ML-powered predictive maintenance and anomaly detection are game-changers for organizations relying on mainframes. These approaches minimize downtime, optimize system performance, and enhance security, ensuring that mainframes continue to deliver reliable and efficient operations.

In the next section, we'll explore **Workload Optimization and Resource Allocation**, detailing how AI/ML models improve system efficiency by dynamically managing resources and balancing workloads.

Workload Optimization and Resource Allocation

Mainframes are engineered to handle vast and varied workloads, often processing millions of transactions per second across multiple applications. However, the unpredictable nature of enterprise demands can lead to resource bottlenecks, inefficient processing, and increased operational costs. AI/ML technologies offer powerful solutions by dynamically optimizing workloads and intelligently allocating resources. This ensures that mainframes operate at peak efficiency, even during periods of high demand.

1. Workload Optimization

Workload optimization involves the intelligent distribution and scheduling of tasks across mainframe resources to maximize performance and minimize bottlenecks. By analyzing workload patterns, AI/ML models can predict resource needs and adjust processing in real-time.

How It Works

1. **Data Collection and Analysis:**
    - **Monitoring Workloads:** AI/ML systems continuously monitor workloads, capturing data on transaction volumes, processing times, resource utilization, and system performance.
    - **Pattern Recognition:** Machine learning algorithms analyze historical and real-time data to identify patterns and trends in workload

demands.

2. **Predictive Modeling:**
    - **Forecasting Demand:** ML models predict future workload spikes or lulls based on historical trends, time of day, seasonality, or external factors (e.g., marketing campaigns).
    - **Identifying Bottlenecks:** The system pinpoints areas where processing delays or resource contention may occur.
3. **Dynamic Adjustment:**
    - **Load Balancing:** AI algorithms redistribute tasks across available resources to ensure an even workload distribution.
    - **Prioritization:** Critical tasks are identified and scheduled appropriately to meet service level agreements (SLAs).

Benefits of Workload Optimization

- **Improved Performance:** Optimized workloads reduce processing times and enhance system responsiveness.
- **Reduced Bottlenecks:** By preventing resource contention, the system operates smoothly even during peak demand.
- **Cost Efficiency:** Efficient workload management minimizes the need for additional hardware investments by maximizing existing resource utilization.

Use Case Example

A global e-commerce company experiences significant traffic fluctuations, especially during promotional events. By implementing AI-driven workload optimization on their mainframe:

- **Challenge:** During flash sales, transaction volumes surge, leading to processing delays and potential system crashes.
- **Solution:** The AI/ML model analyzes traffic patterns and predicts surge periods. It dynamically redistributes workloads, balancing the processing across multiple CPUs and prioritizing transaction processing over less critical background tasks.
- **Result:** The system handles the increased load without downtime, ensuring a seamless customer experience and maximizing sales opportunities.

---

2. Resource Allocation

Resource allocation focuses on distributing mainframe resources—such as CPU time, memory, and I/O bandwidth—to applications and processes based on their priority and requirements. AI/ML models enhance this process by making intelligent, real-time decisions that align with business objectives.

How It Works

1. **Identifying Critical Applications:**
    - **Priority Mapping:** Business-critical applications are identified and assigned higher priorities based on SLAs and operational importance.
    - **Resource Requirements:** The system assesses the resource needs of each application, considering factors like processing power and memory usage.
2. **Real-Time Monitoring:**
    - **Resource Utilization Tracking:** AI/ML models monitor how applications consume resources over time.

    - **Detecting Resource Contention:** The system identifies when multiple applications compete for the same resources.
3. **Dynamic Resource Allocation:**
    - **Intelligent Scheduling:** Resources are allocated dynamically, ensuring critical applications receive the necessary resources when they need them.
    - **Adaptive Scaling:** The system adjusts resource allocation in response to changing workloads and priorities.

Benefits of Resource Allocation

- **Enhanced Performance for Critical Applications:** Ensures that essential services run smoothly without interruptions.
- **Optimal Resource Utilization:** Prevents over-provisioning and under-utilization of resources, reducing operational costs.
- **Improved User Experience:** Applications perform reliably, meeting or exceeding user expectations and SLAs.

Use Case Example

A large banking institution relies on mainframe systems for processing transactions, running risk assessments, and generating reports.

- **Challenge:** During end-of-day processing, batch jobs for report generation compete with transaction processing systems, causing delays.
- **Solution:** The AI/ML model identifies transaction

processing as a higher priority during business hours and allocates more CPU and memory resources to it. Batch jobs are scheduled with lower priority or deferred to off-peak hours.

- **Result:** Transaction processing remains fast and reliable, enhancing customer satisfaction, while reports are generated efficiently without impacting critical operations.

Integration of Workload Optimization and Resource Allocation

While workload optimization focuses on balancing tasks to prevent bottlenecks, resource allocation ensures that the most critical applications have the resources they need. Together, they provide a comprehensive approach to mainframe efficiency:

- **Synergy:** By optimizing workloads and intelligently allocating resources, mainframes operate at peak performance.
- **Adaptability:** AI/ML models adapt to changing workloads and priorities, ensuring continuous alignment with business needs.
- **Scalability:** The system can handle growth in workloads without degradation in performance.

Key Technologies and Techniques

Machine Learning Algorithms:

- **Reinforcement Learning:** Models learn optimal resource allocation strategies through trial and error, improving over time.

- **Predictive Analytics:** Time-series forecasting models predict workload trends and resource demands.

Automation Tools:

- **Intelligent Schedulers:** AI-powered schedulers automate task distribution based on real-time data.
- **Resource Management Software:** Integrates with AI/ML models to adjust resource settings dynamically.

Data Requirements:

- **Historical Workload Data:** Provides the foundation for understanding patterns and training ML models.
- **Real-Time Monitoring Data:** Enables the system to make immediate adjustments based on current conditions.

Challenges and Solutions

Challenge: Complexity of Mainframe Environments

- **Solution:** Use advanced AI/ML models capable of handling complex data structures and dependencies inherent in mainframe systems.

Challenge: Integration with Legacy Systems

- **Solution:** Employ middleware and APIs that facilitate communication between AI/ML models and mainframe operating systems.

Challenge: Ensuring Security and Compliance

- **Solution:** Implement robust security protocols within AI/ML systems and ensure compliance with industry regulations when adjusting workloads and resources.

Conclusion

Workload optimization and resource allocation are critical for maintaining the efficiency and reliability of mainframe systems in today's fast-paced enterprise environments. By leveraging AI/ML technologies, organizations can dynamically adjust to fluctuating demands, prioritize critical applications, and make the most of their mainframe investments.

The intelligent management of workloads and resources not only enhances performance but also drives cost savings and supports business agility. As enterprises continue to evolve, integrating AI/ML into mainframe operations will become increasingly essential for staying competitive and meeting the ever-growing demands of the digital landscape.

In the next section, we'll explore **Enhancing Security and Fraud Detection**, examining how AI/ML models bolster mainframe security by identifying threats and preventing unauthorized activities in real-time.

Enhancing Security and Fraud Detection

Mainframes are the custodians of critical data for enterprises, making them prime targets for cyber threats and fraud. As the scale and sophistication of these threats grow, traditional security measures are no longer sufficient. AI/ML models provide a transformative approach to enhancing security and fraud detection, leveraging their ability to analyze patterns, detect anomalies, and respond proactively in real time.

1. Security: Monitoring Network Traffic and User Activity

AI/ML models bolster mainframe security by continuously monitoring network traffic, user activity, and system logs to identify potential breaches or suspicious behavior. This proactive approach minimizes risks and ensures the integrity of critical systems.

How AI/ML Enhances Security

1. **Baseline Behavior Analysis:**
    - AI/ML systems establish a baseline of normal activity by analyzing historical data, such as user logins, transaction volumes, and access patterns.
    - Example: A model might learn that a specific employee accesses payroll data during working hours but not during weekends or from foreign IP addresses.
2. **Real-Time Monitoring:**
    - Once deployed, AI/ML models continuously monitor network traffic and system activities,

comparing real-time data against the established baseline.
   - Anomalies like unusually high traffic, failed login attempts, or unexpected file access are flagged for further investigation.

3. **Proactive Alerts:**
   - The system generates alerts when suspicious activities are detected, allowing security teams to respond before damage occurs.
   - Example: AI might detect an unauthorized attempt to access customer databases, triggering an immediate account lockout and alert.

Benefits of AI/ML-Enhanced Security

- **Early Threat Detection:** Identifies risks before they escalate into full-scale breaches.
- **Minimized Response Time:** Provides actionable insights to security teams, enabling swift remediation.
- **Reduced False Positives:** AI/ML models refine themselves over time, reducing the noise caused by false alarms.

Use Case Example

A financial institution uses AI/ML to monitor network activity on its mainframe:

- **Challenge:** The institution must prevent unauthorized access to sensitive customer data.
- **Solution:** An ML model identifies a pattern of failed login attempts from an unusual IP address. Upon investigation, the security team discovers and mitigates an attempted

cyberattack.

- **Result:** The breach is stopped before any data is compromised, safeguarding customer trust.

---

2. Fraud Detection: Analyzing Transaction Data

Fraud detection is one of the most critical applications of AI/ML in mainframe environments, particularly in industries like banking, retail, and insurance. Machine learning models excel at identifying patterns indicative of fraudulent activities, even as fraudsters develop increasingly sophisticated tactics.

How AI/ML Enhances Fraud Detection

1. **Pattern Recognition:**
    - ML models analyze transaction histories to identify patterns associated with legitimate behavior. These patterns serve as benchmarks for detecting anomalies.
    - Example: An online retailer's ML model might learn that a customer typically makes purchases within a specific price range and geographic location.
2. **Anomaly Detection:**
    - Deviations from established patterns—such as unusually large transactions, purchases from unfamiliar locations, or rapid successive transactions—trigger fraud alerts.
    - Example: A banking system flags a series of high-value purchases made with a credit card in different countries within a short timeframe.
3. **Real-Time Scoring:**

  - AI models assign fraud risk scores to transactions based on multiple factors, including time, location, and transaction amount.
  - Transactions exceeding a predefined risk threshold can be blocked or flagged for manual review.
4. **Adaptive Learning:**
  - AI/ML systems evolve as they process more data, learning to recognize new fraud tactics and adapting to changing fraud patterns.

Benefits of AI/ML-Enhanced Fraud Detection

- **Increased Accuracy:** AI systems can identify complex, subtle fraud patterns that traditional methods might miss.
- **Scalability:** ML models handle large volumes of transaction data without degradation in performance.
- **Real-Time Response:** Immediate detection and response minimize financial losses and prevent further fraudulent activities.

Use Case Example

A credit card provider integrates an ML-powered fraud detection system into its mainframe:

- **Challenge:** Fraudulent transactions result in significant losses and erode customer trust.
- **Solution:** The AI model detects a high-value transaction initiated from an unfamiliar IP address, followed by an unusually high number of small transactions. The system blocks the transaction and alerts the customer.
- **Result:** The provider saves thousands of dollars in

potential losses and enhances customer confidence in its security measures.

Key Technologies and Techniques

1. AI/ML Algorithms

- **Anomaly Detection Models:** Identify deviations from normal behavior in real-time.
- **Classification Algorithms:** Distinguish between legitimate and fraudulent activities using supervised learning models.

2. Advanced Monitoring Tools

- **Network Behavior Analytics (NBA):** Tracks and analyzes network traffic to detect unusual patterns.
- **User Behavior Analytics (UBA):** Monitors user activity to identify suspicious behaviors, such as login attempts outside of regular working hours.

3. Data Requirements

- **Historical Data:** Provides the foundation for identifying normal behaviors and training fraud detection models.
- **Real-Time Data:** Enables immediate analysis and action against emerging threats.

Challenges and Solutions

Challenge: Balancing Sensitivity and Accuracy

- **Solution:** Regularly retrain AI/ML models to refine their accuracy and reduce false positives.

Challenge: Adapting to Evolving Threats

- **Solution:** Use adaptive learning techniques that allow models to evolve with new fraud tactics and cybersecurity threats.

Challenge: Integration with Legacy Systems

- **Solution:** Employ middleware and APIs to bridge AI/ML systems with mainframe environments seamlessly.

Conclusion

AI/ML technologies revolutionize mainframe security and fraud detection, providing real-time insights and proactive measures to safeguard critical systems and data. By monitoring user activity, analyzing transaction data, and identifying anomalies, AI/ML systems significantly enhance an organization's ability to prevent cyber threats and fraudulent activities.

As cyber threats and fraud tactics evolve, AI/ML's ability to adapt and learn ensures that enterprises stay ahead of emerging risks. In the next section, we'll explore how these technologies enable **Business Benefits of AI/ML Integration**, highlighting cost savings, reliability improvements, and competitive advantages.

7. Business Benefits of AI/ML Integration

The integration of Artificial Intelligence (AI) and Machine Learning (ML) into mainframe environments is not just a technological upgrade; it's a strategic move that delivers measurable business benefits. These benefits extend across cost efficiency, operational reliability, and market competitiveness, making AI/ML a cornerstone of modern enterprise strategies.

In this section, we will explore the tangible advantages of integrating AI/ML into mainframes, highlighting how these technologies drive business success. By examining cost savings, enhanced reliability, competitive edge, and real-world case studies, this chapter will provide a comprehensive understanding of the value AI/ML brings to enterprises.

Overview of Subtopics

1. Cost Savings and Improved Reliability

AI/ML technologies streamline operations, automate repetitive tasks, and optimize resource utilization, all of which translate into significant cost savings. At the same time, these technologies enhance reliability by predicting failures, minimizing downtime, and ensuring consistent performance.

We'll delve into:

- How AI/ML reduces operational expenses by automating processes and improving efficiency.
- The role of predictive maintenance and anomaly detection

in enhancing system uptime and reliability.

---

2. Competitive Advantages Through AI/ML

In today's rapidly evolving business landscape, staying ahead requires leveraging technology to deliver better services, faster decisions, and personalized customer experiences. AI/ML integration allows enterprises to differentiate themselves in the marketplace, driving innovation and building stronger customer relationships.

We'll examine:

- How AI/ML enables data-driven decision-making, accelerates innovation, and enhances customer satisfaction.
- The role of AI/ML in creating scalable and adaptable systems that support long-term growth.

---

3. Case Studies of Successful Implementations

Nothing illustrates the potential of AI/ML integration better than real-world success stories. This subtopic will showcase enterprises that have effectively implemented AI/ML in their mainframe environments, highlighting their challenges, solutions, and results.

We'll explore:

- Specific industries and organizations that have achieved measurable benefits through AI/ML adoption.
- Key takeaways from these implementations that can inform your enterprise's AI/ML journey.

Conclusion

Integrating AI/ML into mainframes isn't just about modernizing systems—it's about transforming the way businesses operate, compete, and grow. In the following sections, we will detail the specific benefits, from cost savings and reliability improvements to competitive advantages and real-world success stories.

Let's start by exploring how AI/ML integration drives **Cost Savings and Improved Reliability**, setting the stage for the broader business benefits of these transformative technologies.

Cost Savings and Improved Reliability

The integration of AI/ML into mainframe environments delivers substantial financial and operational advantages. By streamlining processes, automating repetitive tasks, and enhancing resource utilization, these technologies reduce operational expenses while improving overall system performance. Simultaneously, AI/ML bolsters reliability by identifying potential failures before they occur and minimizing downtime, ensuring uninterrupted service.

Reducing Operational Expenses

AI/ML technologies enable enterprises to cut costs by automating manual processes, optimizing resource usage, and improving decision-making efficiency.

How AI/ML Reduces Costs

1. **Automation of Repetitive Tasks**
    - **Challenge:** Manual processes are labor-intensive, time-consuming, and prone to errors.
    - **Solution:** AI-powered systems automate tasks such as data entry, report generation, compliance checks, and transaction validation.
    - **Example:** A financial institution uses AI to automate loan approval processes, reducing processing time from days to minutes while lowering labor costs.
2. **Optimized Resource Utilization**
    - **Challenge:** Underutilized or misallocated resources can lead to wasted operational spending.

    - **Solution:** AI/ML models analyze workload patterns and adjust resource allocation dynamically to prevent overprovisioning or underutilization.
    - **Example:** AI-driven resource management allows a retail company to allocate server capacity based on predicted traffic, saving energy costs during low-demand periods.
3. **Improved Decision-Making**
    - **Challenge:** Inefficient decision-making leads to unnecessary spending and operational delays.
    - **Solution:** AI-powered analytics provide actionable insights, enabling organizations to make faster, data-driven decisions.
    - **Example:** An e-commerce platform uses AI to analyze customer purchase patterns, optimizing inventory levels and reducing excess stock storage costs.

Benefits

- **Labor Cost Savings:** Automation reduces the need for manual intervention, freeing up personnel for higher-value tasks.
- **Energy Efficiency:** Optimized resource usage lowers energy consumption, contributing to both cost savings and sustainability goals.
- **Increased Productivity:** Faster processes and fewer errors result in more efficient operations.

Enhancing Reliability

AI/ML technologies significantly enhance system reliability by leveraging predictive maintenance and anomaly detection to prevent failures and ensure consistent performance.

The Role of Predictive Maintenance

1. **Proactive Issue Identification**
    - AI/ML models analyze historical performance data to identify patterns that indicate potential hardware or software issues.
    - Example: Predictive maintenance alerts a logistics company to impending disk failures on its mainframe, enabling preemptive replacements and avoiding costly downtime.
2. **Minimized Unplanned Downtime**
    - By addressing issues before they escalate, AI/ML reduces the frequency and duration of outages.
    - Example: A telecom provider uses ML to monitor server temperatures and prevent overheating, ensuring uninterrupted service for customers.
3. **Cost-Efficient Maintenance Scheduling**
    - AI/ML schedules maintenance activities during low-demand periods, minimizing disruption to operations.
    - Example: A bank schedules database optimizations during off-peak hours, avoiding impact on customer transactions.

The Role of Anomaly Detection

1. **Real-Time Monitoring**
    - AI models continuously monitor system logs, resource usage, and network traffic for deviations

from normal patterns.
   - Example: A healthcare organization uses anomaly detection to identify unusual spikes in mainframe CPU usage, resolving issues before they affect patient data access.
2. **Improved Security and Stability**
   - Anomalies often signal underlying security risks or system inefficiencies. Detecting and resolving them promptly prevents larger issues.
   - Example: A government agency detects unauthorized access attempts to its mainframe through real-time AI monitoring, mitigating potential breaches.
3. **Continuous System Optimization**
   - AI/ML systems learn from identified anomalies to refine their detection capabilities over time.

Benefits

- **Enhanced System Uptime:** Predictive maintenance and anomaly detection ensure mainframes remain operational with minimal disruptions.
- **Reduced Repair Costs:** Early issue detection prevents minor problems from escalating into costly failures.
- **Improved User Experience:** Reliable systems enhance customer satisfaction and trust.

Integration of Cost Savings and Reliability

AI/ML technologies achieve a dual benefit by reducing costs and improving reliability simultaneously. For example:

- Predictive maintenance lowers repair costs while ensuring uninterrupted service.
- Automation reduces manual labor expenses while minimizing the risk of human error.
- Resource optimization reduces energy usage while maintaining consistent performance during peak periods.

Conclusion

The cost savings and reliability enhancements offered by AI/ML integration make a compelling case for adopting these technologies in mainframe environments. By automating processes, optimizing resources, and proactively addressing system issues, organizations can achieve operational excellence while reducing expenses.

In the next section, we'll explore **Competitive Advantages Through AI/ML**, examining how these technologies enable enterprises to differentiate themselves in the market, drive innovation, and deliver superior customer experiences.

Competitive Advantages Through AI/ ML

In a business environment shaped by technological advancements and shifting customer expectations, the ability to innovate and adapt is key to maintaining a competitive edge. AI/ML technologies provide enterprises with powerful tools to deliver exceptional services, make faster and smarter decisions, and meet customer demands with personalized solutions. By integrating AI/ML into mainframe environments, organizations can transform these foundational systems into engines of growth and differentiation.

1. Data-Driven Decision-Making, Accelerated Innovation, and Enhanced Customer Satisfaction

AI/ML integration enhances an organization's ability to leverage its data, innovate rapidly, and provide value-driven customer experiences. These benefits establish a strong competitive position in the marketplace.

Data-Driven Decision-Making

AI/ML systems analyze vast amounts of structured and unstructured data, uncovering patterns and trends that drive informed decision-making.

- **How It Works:**
  - Machine learning models process historical and real-time data to predict outcomes, identify risks, and recommend optimal courses of action.
  - Example: A financial services firm uses ML

models on its mainframe to simulate various market scenarios, optimizing investment strategies for better portfolio performance.

- **Business Impact:**
  - Faster, more accurate decisions improve efficiency and reduce operational uncertainty.
  - Insights from AI/ML systems allow organizations to respond proactively to changes in market conditions.

Accelerated Innovation

AI/ML integration fosters innovation by automating routine tasks, freeing up resources for creative problem-solving, and enabling experimentation with new technologies.

- **How It Works:**
  - AI systems automate processes like fraud detection, anomaly reporting, and inventory forecasting, allowing human teams to focus on innovation.
  - Example: A retail company integrates AI on its mainframe to test new pricing strategies based on real-time market data.
- **Business Impact:**
  - Faster innovation cycles keep organizations ahead of competitors.
  - AI-driven insights enable the development of novel products, services, and solutions tailored to emerging customer needs.

Enhanced Customer Satisfaction

Personalized experiences and faster service are essential for building customer loyalty. AI/ML enables enterprises to exceed expectations through predictive analytics and tailored interactions.

- **How It Works:**
    - Machine learning models analyze customer behavior to deliver personalized recommendations, targeted promotions, and real-time support.
    - Example: An airline uses AI-powered chatbots integrated with its mainframe to provide instant customer service, reducing wait times and improving satisfaction.
- **Business Impact:**
    - Enhanced customer experiences lead to higher retention rates and brand loyalty.
    - Predictive models enable proactive engagement, such as alerting customers about service disruptions or offering tailored solutions.

---

2. Scalable and Adaptable Systems for Long-Term Growth

AI/ML technologies enhance the scalability and adaptability of enterprise systems, ensuring that organizations can handle growth and evolve with market demands.

Scalable Systems

AI/ML integration allows mainframes to handle increasing workloads, expanding seamlessly as the business grows.

- **How It Works:**
    - AI-powered resource management ensures

efficient utilization of existing infrastructure while scaling to accommodate higher demand.
    - Example: A healthcare organization uses AI on its mainframe to scale patient data processing as its network of hospitals expands.
- **Business Impact:**
    - Improved scalability ensures operational continuity during growth phases.
    - Organizations avoid the cost and disruption of frequent infrastructure upgrades.

Adaptable Systems

AI/ML systems continuously learn and improve, enabling organizations to adapt to new challenges and opportunities.

- **How It Works:**
    - Machine learning models refine themselves based on new data, improving their predictions and recommendations over time.
    - Example: A logistics company uses adaptive AI models on its mainframe to adjust delivery schedules in response to changing traffic patterns or weather conditions.
- **Business Impact:**
    - Adaptable systems allow enterprises to respond quickly to changing market conditions, regulatory requirements, and customer preferences.
    - Long-term adaptability positions organizations as leaders in innovation and resilience.

Key Benefits of Competitive AI/ML Integration

1. **Differentiation in the Marketplace:**
    - Deliver unique services, such as real-time fraud prevention or hyper-personalized customer experiences, that set your organization apart.
2. **Enhanced Operational Efficiency:**
    - AI/ML streamlines processes, reduces waste, and enables cost-effective scaling, freeing up resources for strategic initiatives.
3. **Proactive Problem-Solving:**
    - AI/ML technologies allow organizations to identify and address challenges before they escalate, maintaining a competitive edge.
4. **Sustainable Growth:**
    - AI/ML enables mainframes to evolve with the business, ensuring they remain relevant and impactful in a changing landscape.

Examples of Competitive Advantage in Action

- **Financial Sector:**
  A global bank uses AI/ML models on its mainframe to provide real-time credit scoring and fraud detection, differentiating itself by offering faster and more secure financial services.
- **Retail Industry:**
  A leading retailer integrates AI into its mainframe to deliver dynamic pricing and inventory management, increasing profit margins while enhancing customer satisfaction with availability.
- **Healthcare:**
  A hospital network employs AI-powered predictive

analytics to improve patient outcomes, creating a competitive advantage by positioning itself as a leader in personalized medicine.

Conclusion

AI/ML integration is not just a technical enhancement—it's a strategic enabler of competitive advantage. By enabling data-driven decisions, accelerating innovation, and creating scalable, adaptable systems, these technologies position enterprises for long-term success.

In the next section, we'll explore **Case Studies of Successful Implementations**, providing real-world examples of how AI/ML has driven transformative benefits in enterprises across industries.

Case Studies of Successful Implementations

Real-world examples provide the most compelling evidence of the transformative potential of AI/ML integration. By examining how organizations across various industries have embraced these technologies in their mainframe environments, we gain actionable insights into overcoming challenges and maximizing benefits.

This section highlights enterprises that have achieved measurable success with AI/ML integration, focusing on their initial challenges, innovative solutions, and resulting outcomes. These case studies also offer valuable takeaways to guide your own AI/ML journey.

1. Financial Services: Real-Time Fraud Detection

Challenge:

A global bank faced increasing incidents of fraudulent transactions. Its existing rule-based systems struggled to keep up with evolving fraud tactics, leading to financial losses and diminished customer trust.

Solution:

The bank implemented an AI/ML-powered fraud detection system integrated with its mainframe environment.

- **ML Models Used:** Supervised learning models trained on historical transaction data to identify fraudulent patterns.
- **Implementation:** Real-time monitoring of transactions

for anomalies, such as unusual purchase amounts or locations.

Results:

- Fraud detection accuracy improved by 40%, with false positives reduced by 25%.
- The system identified suspicious transactions within milliseconds, enabling immediate action to block unauthorized activities.
- Customer trust was restored through improved security measures.

Key Takeaway:

AI/ML integration enables proactive fraud prevention by adapting to new patterns of fraudulent behavior, delivering both operational efficiency and customer confidence.

---

2. Retail: Dynamic Pricing and Inventory Management

Challenge:

A leading retailer struggled with stockouts and overstocking due to inaccurate demand forecasts, which increased storage costs and led to missed sales opportunities.

Solution:

The company deployed AI/ML models on its mainframe to predict demand and optimize pricing dynamically.

- **ML Models Used:** Time-series forecasting for demand prediction and reinforcement learning for pricing adjustments.

- **Implementation:** Real-time analysis of customer data, market trends, and competitor pricing.

Results:

- Stockouts decreased by 30%, and overstocking was reduced by 20%, saving millions in storage costs.
- Profit margins increased by 15% due to optimized pricing strategies.
- Customer satisfaction improved as products were consistently available during peak demand periods.

Key Takeaway:

AI/ML models can drive profitability and operational efficiency by transforming how inventory and pricing decisions are made.

---

3. Healthcare: Predictive Analytics for Patient Care

Challenge:

A hospital network faced challenges in managing patient care resources, such as beds and medical staff, during peak periods. Inefficiencies led to delayed treatments and reduced patient satisfaction.

Solution:

The network integrated predictive analytics powered by AI/ML into its mainframe systems to forecast patient demand and optimize resource allocation.

- **ML Models Used:** Supervised learning models trained on historical patient admission data and external factors such as seasonal trends.

- **Implementation:** Real-time dashboards provided actionable insights into resource needs across facilities.

Results:

- Emergency room wait times decreased by 25%, improving patient outcomes and satisfaction.
- Staff schedules were optimized, reducing overtime costs by 15%.
- Patient admission planning improved, increasing bed utilization efficiency by 20%.

Key Takeaway:

AI/ML integration can enhance service delivery and operational efficiency in industries requiring precise resource management.

4. Manufacturing: Predictive Maintenance

Challenge:

A manufacturing company faced costly unplanned downtime due to equipment failures. Traditional maintenance schedules were inefficient, often resulting in either unnecessary maintenance or missed failure warnings.

Solution:

The company implemented predictive maintenance using AI/ML models on its mainframe.

- **ML Models Used:** Anomaly detection models trained on sensor data from machinery.
- **Implementation:** Continuous monitoring of equipment performance to predict failures and recommend

maintenance schedules.

Results:

- Unplanned downtime decreased by 40%, saving millions in lost productivity.
- Maintenance costs were reduced by 25% as resources were allocated only when needed.
- Equipment lifespan increased by 15% due to timely interventions.

Key Takeaway:

Predictive maintenance powered by AI/ML ensures operational continuity while reducing maintenance costs and extending asset life.

---

5. Government: Data Security and Compliance

Challenge:

A government agency faced rising cybersecurity threats targeting sensitive citizen data stored on mainframes. Existing security systems were reactive and insufficient to address sophisticated attacks.

Solution:

The agency integrated AI/ML-based anomaly detection models into its mainframe security infrastructure.

- **ML Models Used:** Supervised and unsupervised learning models to identify abnormal user activity and network traffic patterns.
- **Implementation:** Real-time alerts for unauthorized access attempts and unusual data transfer volumes.

Results:

- Cybersecurity threats were identified and mitigated 50% faster.
- Data breaches were reduced to near-zero incidents within the first year of implementation.
- Compliance with data protection regulations improved significantly, avoiding potential penalties.

Key Takeaway:

AI/ML integration strengthens security frameworks, providing proactive defense mechanisms against evolving cyber threats.

Cross-Industry Insights

Shared Challenges and Solutions

Challenge	AI/ML Solution	Outcome
Evolving Threats	Adaptive ML models	Real-time fraud detection and enhanced security
Demand Volatility	Predictive analytics	Optimized inventory and resource planning
Operational Inefficiencies	Automation and workload optimization	Cost savings and improved reliability

Conclusion

These case studies demonstrate the tangible benefits of AI/ML integration in mainframe environments across industries. From preventing fraud and optimizing operations to enhancing customer experiences and improving security, these success stories highlight the transformative potential of these technologies.

Part III: Preparing Your Mainframe Environment for AI/ML

Integrating Artificial Intelligence (AI) and Machine Learning (ML) into mainframe environments requires more than just adopting new technologies; it demands thoughtful preparation and strategic planning. The foundation of a successful AI/ML initiative lies in thoroughly understanding your current system, defining clear objectives, and charting a roadmap to guide the transformation journey.

Part III focuses on the critical preparatory steps organizations must take to ensure their mainframe systems are ready to embrace AI/ML capabilities. These steps involve evaluating the existing environment, aligning modernization goals with business priorities, and crafting a structured plan for implementation. By addressing these elements, enterprises can set the stage for seamless integration and long-term success.

What This Section Covers

Assessing the Current State

Before embarking on an AI/ML integration journey, it's essential to gain a comprehensive understanding of your mainframe environment. This involves identifying strengths, weaknesses, and opportunities for improvement. A detailed audit ensures that modernization efforts are grounded in data and tailored to the unique needs of the system.

Aligning Goals with Strategy

Every modernization effort should serve a larger purpose. Defining clear, measurable objectives ensures that AI/ML initiatives align with organizational goals, whether it's improving efficiency, enhancing customer experiences, or driving innovation. This alignment provides a sense of direction and prioritization.

Building a Path Forward

A strategic roadmap translates goals into actionable steps, breaking down the complexity of AI/ML integration into manageable phases. This plan ensures that the transition is systematic, minimizes risks, and delivers incremental value throughout the process.

Why Preparation Matters

The preparation phase is crucial for mitigating risks, optimizing resource allocation, and ensuring that AI/ML integration delivers its full potential. By addressing gaps in the current system, defining objectives, and creating a detailed roadmap, organizations can avoid common pitfalls and set themselves up for success.

This part of the book will guide you through each step of the preparation process, offering actionable insights and practical strategies to help your organization take the first steps toward AI/ML-enabled transformation.

8. Conducting a Mainframe System Audit

Preparing your mainframe environment for AI/ML integration begins with a thorough assessment of its current state. A comprehensive system audit is a critical first step in understanding the strengths, weaknesses, and readiness of your infrastructure. This process not only identifies areas for improvement but also lays the foundation for strategic decision-making in modernization efforts.

In this chapter, we'll explore the tools, techniques, and best practices for auditing a mainframe system, focusing on two key aspects: assessing system performance and identifying bottlenecks and opportunities. A successful audit will empower your organization with the insights needed to align its mainframe environment with AI/ML integration requirements.

Overview of Subtopics

1. Tools and Techniques for Assessing System Performance

Auditing a mainframe requires leveraging the right tools and methodologies to gather meaningful data on its operations. This subtopic will explore:

- The software and utilities available for monitoring key performance metrics, such as CPU usage, memory utilization, I/O efficiency, and transaction processing times.
- Techniques for analyzing historical and real-time data to identify trends and patterns that impact performance.

- Best practices for creating a performance baseline to benchmark future improvements and measure the impact of AI/ML integration.

By mastering these tools and techniques, you'll gain a comprehensive understanding of how well your mainframe is performing and where optimization efforts should be focused.

2. Identifying Bottlenecks and Opportunities

Once system performance data is gathered, the next step is to interpret it to uncover areas of concern and potential growth. This subtopic will cover:

- Common bottlenecks in mainframe environments, such as processing delays, resource contention, and inefficient workloads.
- Methods for pinpointing underperforming components, applications, or processes that hinder overall system efficiency.
- Opportunities for modernization, including upgrading outdated infrastructure, improving resource allocation, and integrating automation.

By identifying bottlenecks and opportunities, your organization can prioritize efforts that yield the highest impact, ensuring a smoother transition to AI/ML-enabled operations.

Conclusion

A mainframe system audit is more than a technical exercise; it's a strategic process that provides the clarity needed to align modernization efforts with business objectives. In this chapter, you'll learn how to effectively assess your system's performance and uncover actionable insights to guide your AI/ML integration journey.

Next, we'll delve deeper into **Tools and Techniques for Assessing System Performance**, exploring how to gather and analyze critical data to understand your mainframe's capabilities.

Tools and Techniques for Assessing System Performance

Conducting a mainframe system audit is a crucial step in preparing for AI/ML integration. Effective auditing depends on using the right tools and methodologies to measure performance and identify areas of improvement. By leveraging these tools and techniques, organizations can establish a clear picture of their mainframe's current capabilities and its readiness for modernization.

1. Software and Utilities for Monitoring Key Performance Metrics

The first step in assessing system performance is to gather meaningful data on critical performance metrics. A variety of specialized tools and utilities are available to monitor and analyze mainframe operations, providing valuable insights into system efficiency.

Key Metrics to Monitor

- **CPU Usage:** Tracks processor utilization to identify potential overuse or inefficiencies.
- **Memory Utilization:** Monitors memory allocation to ensure that resources are neither overcommitted nor underutilized.
- **I/O Efficiency:** Evaluates the performance of input/output operations, detecting bottlenecks in data transfer.
- **Transaction Processing Times:** Measures the speed and reliability of application transactions, highlighting delays or failures.

Recommended Tools

- **IBM z/OS Resource Measurement Facility (RMF):**
  A robust tool for monitoring and reporting on mainframe system performance, offering detailed insights into CPU, memory, and I/O utilization.
- **MainView by BMC:**
  Provides a real-time view of mainframe performance, enabling proactive issue resolution.
- **Splunk for Mainframes:**
  Combines data analytics with monitoring, offering advanced capabilities for performance visualization and anomaly detection.
- **Perfmon (Performance Monitor):**
  Useful for tracking specific metrics and creating customized reports.

---

2. Techniques for Analyzing Historical and Real-Time Data

Once data is collected, the next step is to analyze it effectively. Both historical and real-time data are valuable for understanding system behavior and identifying performance trends.

Historical Data Analysis

- **Purpose:**
  Historical data provides insights into past performance trends, recurring issues, and seasonal workload patterns.
- **Techniques:**
  - Use data visualization tools to identify patterns in resource usage over time.
  - Perform root cause analysis on past outages or

inefficiencies to prevent recurrence.

- **Example:**
  Historical data analysis might reveal that transaction processing times spike during end-of-quarter reporting, signaling the need for workload optimization.

Real-Time Data Analysis

- **Purpose:**
  Real-time monitoring ensures that potential issues are identified and resolved immediately, preventing disruptions.
- **Techniques:**
    - Implement dashboards for continuous performance visualization.
    - Use anomaly detection algorithms to flag deviations from expected behavior.
- **Example:**
  Real-time monitoring might detect an unexpected surge in CPU usage, allowing operators to reallocate resources before it affects application performance.

---

3. Best Practices for Creating a Performance Baseline

A performance baseline is a critical reference point for benchmarking system improvements and measuring the impact of AI/ML integration.

Steps to Create a Baseline

1. **Identify Key Metrics:**
   Determine which metrics are most relevant to your

mainframe's operations, such as throughput, latency, and error rates.

2. **Collect Data Over Time:**
   Gather data during normal operating conditions to ensure that the baseline represents typical performance.
3. **Incorporate Variability:**
   Account for fluctuations in workload, such as seasonal spikes or specific business events.
4. **Document Results:**
   Record the baseline data in a centralized location for easy reference during future audits.

Benefits of a Performance Baseline

- **Improvement Tracking:**
  Allows organizations to measure progress over time and validate the effectiveness of optimization efforts.
- **Problem Diagnosis:**
  Serves as a reference point for identifying deviations in system performance.
- **AI/ML Integration Impact:**
  Provides a clear benchmark to evaluate how AI/ML technologies improve key metrics after deployment.

Practical Application

Example Audit Workflow

1. **Set Objectives:**
   Define the goals of the audit, such as identifying bottlenecks or establishing readiness for AI/ML integration.

2. **Choose Tools:**
   Select the appropriate tools for data collection and monitoring based on the metrics of interest.
3. **Collect Data:**
   Use the tools to gather historical and real-time data on system performance.
4. **Analyze Results:**
   Interpret the data to identify trends, anomalies, and areas for improvement.
5. **Establish Baseline:**
   Create a performance baseline and document findings to inform modernization strategies.

Conclusion

Assessing mainframe system performance is an essential step in preparing for AI/ML integration. By using specialized tools and employing robust analysis techniques, organizations can gain actionable insights into their systems' operations. A well-executed audit ensures that optimization efforts are targeted and effective, paving the way for a successful modernization journey.

In the next section, we will explore **Identifying Bottlenecks and Opportunities**, diving into how to pinpoint underperforming components and uncover potential areas for growth within your mainframe environment.

Identifying Bottlenecks and Opportunities

With comprehensive system performance data in hand, the next critical step is interpreting that data to identify bottlenecks and uncover opportunities for optimization and modernization. This analysis ensures that your mainframe environment is not only ready for AI/ML integration but also positioned for improved efficiency, reliability, and scalability.

1. Common Bottlenecks in Mainframe Environments

Mainframe systems are robust but complex, and various factors can impede their performance. Identifying these bottlenecks is key to unlocking their full potential.

Processing Delays

- **Symptoms:** Long transaction processing times, frequent slowdowns during peak loads, or delayed responses to user queries.
- **Causes:** Inefficient algorithms, excessive workload, or outdated hardware components.
- **Impact:** Reduced system throughput, dissatisfied users, and potential financial losses during critical operations.

Resource Contention

- **Symptoms:** High CPU utilization, memory shortages, or disk I/O congestion when multiple processes compete for limited resources.

- **Causes:** Poor workload distribution, misconfigured system priorities, or underprovisioned resources.
- **Impact:** Reduced system reliability and increased risk of unplanned downtime.

Inefficient Workloads

- **Symptoms:** High variability in system performance, underutilized system components, or jobs that fail to complete within expected timelines.
- **Causes:** Suboptimal scheduling, redundant tasks, or poorly optimized applications.
- **Impact:** Increased operational costs and wasted system capacity.

---

2. Methods for Pinpointing Underperforming Components, Applications, or Processes

Once bottlenecks are identified, the next step is isolating the specific areas responsible for these inefficiencies. This process requires detailed analysis and targeted troubleshooting.

Analyzing Component Performance

- **How to Detect:**
  - Use tools like IBM z/OS RMF or MainView to measure CPU, memory, and I/O usage.
  - Identify components operating near or beyond their capacity limits.
- **Example:** High CPU utilization during batch processing may indicate an underperforming database query or poorly optimized application logic.

Evaluating Applications

- **How to Detect:**
  - Analyze application logs for errors, timeouts, or excessive resource consumption.
  - Monitor response times for user-facing applications to identify latency issues.
- **Example:** A customer service portal experiencing slow response times may signal an inefficient API integration with the mainframe.

Examining Workflows and Processes

- **How to Detect:**
  - Review workload distribution patterns and job scheduling effectiveness.
  - Identify redundant or overlapping processes that consume unnecessary resources.
- **Example:** A payroll process that runs during peak business hours may compete for resources, causing delays in other critical operations.

---

3. Opportunities for Modernization

Once bottlenecks are identified, organizations can prioritize improvements that deliver the most value. This involves evaluating opportunities for modernization across various aspects of the mainframe environment.

Upgrading Outdated Infrastructure

- **Opportunities:**
  - Replace legacy hardware with modern alternatives

  to improve performance and energy efficiency.
  - Upgrade storage systems to support higher throughput and lower latency.
- **Example:** Transitioning from traditional disk storage to SSDs can significantly reduce I/O bottlenecks during high-demand periods.

Improving Resource Allocation

- **Opportunities:**
  - Implement dynamic resource allocation to adjust to workload fluctuations in real-time.
  - Use AI-driven resource management tools to optimize utilization.
- **Example:** AI/ML models can redistribute system resources to prioritize mission-critical applications during peak loads.

Integrating Automation

- **Opportunities:**
  - Automate repetitive tasks, such as batch processing, error resolution, or system backups.
  - Use automation to monitor and resolve minor issues before they escalate.
- **Example:** Automated anomaly detection systems can flag and resolve network traffic spikes without manual intervention.

Prioritizing Improvements

Not all bottlenecks and opportunities are equal in terms of impact. Prioritization ensures that modernization efforts yield the highest returns.

Key Considerations:

- **Business Impact:** Address issues that directly affect critical operations or customer experiences.
- **Cost vs. Benefit:** Focus on improvements that offer the most significant ROI with minimal disruption.
- **Scalability:** Prioritize solutions that support long-term growth and evolving workloads.

Practical Example

Scenario: Retail Organization

- **Bottleneck:** Frequent transaction delays during seasonal sales due to resource contention.
- **Analysis:** Performance data reveals high CPU usage caused by poorly optimized pricing algorithms.
- **Opportunity:** Upgrade the pricing engine and implement AI/ML-based resource management to dynamically allocate resources during peak periods.
- **Result:** Transaction speeds improve by 30%, leading to higher customer satisfaction and increased sales revenue.

Conclusion

Identifying bottlenecks and opportunities in mainframe environments is a critical step in preparing for AI/ML integration. By addressing inefficiencies and embracing modernization, organizations can transform their mainframes into agile, high-performing systems ready to support advanced technologies.

Next, we will delve into **Defining Your Modernization Goals**, exploring how to align AI/ML initiatives with your organization's strategic objectives and business priorities.

9. Defining Your Modernization Goals

Establishing clear modernization goals is a vital step in ensuring the successful integration of AI/ML into your mainframe environment. These goals serve as a strategic guide, helping you focus efforts on initiatives that align with your business priorities and deliver the greatest value. Without well-defined objectives, organizations risk implementing technology for technology's sake, leading to wasted resources and missed opportunities.

In this chapter, we will explore how to define and refine your modernization goals, ensuring they are both actionable and aligned with your organization's long-term vision. By linking AI/ML initiatives to business needs and strategically prioritizing projects, you can maximize impact and set the stage for a smooth transformation.

Overview of Subtopics

1. Aligning AI/ML Objectives with Business Needs

AI/ML integration must be driven by clear business objectives, ensuring that technology adoption directly supports organizational goals. This subtopic will discuss:

- **Understanding Business Priorities:** How to identify the key drivers of success in your organization, such as cost reduction, improved customer experiences, or operational efficiency.
- **Translating Business Needs into AI/ML Goals:** How to align AI/ML capabilities—such as predictive analytics,

automation, and real-time decision-making—with these priorities.
- **Examples of Alignment:** Real-world scenarios where AI/ML adoption has driven measurable business outcomes, such as increased revenue or enhanced security.

By aligning AI/ML initiatives with business needs, you ensure that every modernization effort has a purpose and delivers tangible benefits.

---

2. Prioritizing Projects Based on Impact and Feasibility

Once objectives are aligned, it's essential to determine which projects to tackle first. This subtopic will cover:

- **Evaluating Impact:** How to assess the potential value of a project in terms of cost savings, efficiency gains, or competitive advantage.
- **Assessing Feasibility:** How to evaluate the complexity, resource requirements, and risks associated with each initiative.
- **Creating a Prioritization Framework:** How to rank projects based on their impact-to-effort ratio, ensuring that high-value, low-complexity initiatives are addressed first.

This structured approach allows organizations to allocate resources effectively, avoid overextension, and achieve quick wins that build momentum for broader transformation.

Why Defining Modernization Goals Matters

Defining modernization goals is not just about setting a direction—it's about ensuring alignment, focus, and measurable success. Clear objectives and prioritized initiatives enable organizations to:

- **Optimize Resources:** Allocate time, budget, and talent where they will have the most impact.
- **Mitigate Risks:** Avoid the pitfalls of misaligned or overly ambitious projects.
- **Drive Results:** Ensure that AI/ML integration delivers real, actionable benefits.

By the end of this chapter, you will have the tools and insights needed to define modernization goals that are aligned with your organization's strategic vision and poised to deliver measurable outcomes.

Next, we'll dive deeper into **Aligning AI/ML Objectives with Business Needs**, examining how to link technology initiatives with your organization's key success factors.

Aligning AI/ML Objectives with Business Needs

Integrating AI/ML into mainframe environments is not just a technological upgrade; it's a strategic initiative that must directly address an organization's business priorities. Without clear alignment, even the most advanced AI/ML solutions can fall short of delivering meaningful impact. This section explores how to align AI/ML objectives with business needs, ensuring that every effort serves a well-defined purpose and contributes to measurable outcomes.

1. Understanding Business Priorities

The foundation of aligning AI/ML objectives lies in understanding what drives success in your organization. Business priorities vary across industries and enterprises, but the process of identifying them follows similar principles.

Key Business Drivers

- **Cost Reduction:**
  Organizations often seek to reduce operational expenses, whether by streamlining processes, automating tasks, or optimizing resource allocation.
  - **Example:** A financial institution may prioritize cost savings by automating routine compliance checks using AI.
- **Improved Customer Experiences:**
  Delivering faster, more personalized, and reliable services can enhance customer satisfaction and retention.
  - **Example:** A retail company might focus on deploying AI-

powered recommendation engines to improve online shopping experiences.

- **Operational Efficiency:**
  Organizations aim to eliminate bottlenecks, reduce downtime, and maximize productivity.
  - **Example:** A manufacturing company may prioritize predictive maintenance to minimize disruptions in production.

Steps to Identify Priorities

1. **Stakeholder Engagement:** Collaborate with key stakeholders across departments to understand their pain points and objectives.
2. **Data Analysis:** Examine historical performance metrics, customer feedback, and financial reports to identify areas needing improvement.
3. **Strategic Alignment:** Ensure that identified priorities align with the broader organizational goals, such as growth targets or market positioning.

---

2. Translating Business Needs into AI/ML Goals

Once business priorities are identified, the next step is to translate them into actionable AI/ML objectives. This involves mapping AI/ML capabilities to specific organizational needs.

Key AI/ML Capabilities

- **Predictive Analytics:**
  AI/ML models analyze historical and real-time data to predict outcomes, enabling proactive decision-making.
  - **Alignment Example:** Predictive analytics can address a

priority of reducing operational downtime by forecasting potential system failures.

- **Automation:**
  AI-powered systems automate repetitive tasks, improving accuracy and freeing up human resources for strategic initiatives.
    - **Alignment Example:** Automating invoice processing can align with a goal to cut administrative costs.
- **Real-Time Decision-Making:**
  Machine learning models process data in real time to deliver instant insights, enabling rapid responses to dynamic situations.
    - **Alignment Example:** Real-time fraud detection aligns with a financial institution's need to enhance security and customer trust.

Practical Steps for Alignment

1. **Define Specific Goals:** Break down business priorities into specific, measurable objectives (e.g., "reduce downtime by 20% in six months").
2. **Select Relevant Capabilities:** Choose AI/ML tools and techniques that directly address these objectives.
3. **Establish Metrics:** Identify KPIs (Key Performance Indicators) to measure progress, such as cost savings, customer satisfaction scores, or system uptime.

---

3. Examples of Alignment

Real-world examples highlight how organizations can effectively align AI/ML initiatives with their business needs.

Example 1: Financial Services – Fraud Detection

- **Business Priority:** Enhance security and reduce financial losses from fraudulent activities.
- **AI/ML Objective:** Implement a machine learning model to detect unusual transaction patterns.
- **Outcome:** Fraud detection accuracy improved by 40%, and false positives decreased by 25%, directly enhancing customer trust and reducing costs.

Example 2: Retail – Personalized Marketing

- **Business Priority:** Increase revenue through improved customer engagement.
- **AI/ML Objective:** Use AI-powered recommendation engines to personalize marketing campaigns.
- **Outcome:** Conversion rates improved by 15%, leading to a significant increase in revenue.

Example 3: Manufacturing – Predictive Maintenance

- **Business Priority:** Minimize production downtime and optimize resource utilization.
- **AI/ML Objective:** Deploy predictive maintenance models to identify potential equipment failures.
- **Outcome:** Unplanned downtime was reduced by 40%, and maintenance costs decreased by 25%.

Key Benefits of Alignment

Aligning AI/ML objectives with business needs ensures:

- **Purposeful Modernization:** Every initiative contributes to tangible, measurable outcomes.
- **Resource Optimization:** Efforts are focused on projects that deliver the highest value.
- **Enhanced Buy-In:** Stakeholders across the organization can see the direct benefits of AI/ML adoption, increasing support and collaboration.

Conclusion

Aligning AI/ML initiatives with business priorities is a critical step in modernization efforts. By understanding organizational needs, translating them into specific AI/ML goals, and learning from successful implementations, enterprises can ensure that their technology investments deliver meaningful and measurable value.

Next, we will explore **Prioritizing Projects Based on Impact and Feasibility**, focusing on how to select and sequence AI/ML initiatives to maximize results.

Prioritizing Projects Based on Impact and Feasibility

Once your organization has aligned its AI/ML objectives with business needs, the next step is to decide which projects to tackle first. Not all initiatives are equal in terms of potential value and complexity, so prioritizing effectively ensures resources are allocated where they can deliver the greatest impact. A structured approach to prioritization allows organizations to achieve quick wins, build momentum, and reduce risks as they modernize their mainframe environments.

1. Evaluating Impact

The potential value of a project should be the first consideration in prioritization. Understanding how an initiative contributes to business goals ensures that efforts are focused on delivering meaningful outcomes.

Criteria for Assessing Impact

- **Cost Savings:**
  Evaluate how much the initiative can reduce operational expenses.
  - **Example:** Implementing AI-driven workload optimization to decrease energy consumption and hardware wear.
- **Efficiency Gains:**
  Determine how the project improves productivity or system performance.
  - **Example:** Using predictive maintenance to minimize unplanned downtime and streamline operations.

- **Competitive Advantage:**
  Assess how the initiative positions the organization ahead of competitors.
    - **Example:** Deploying AI-powered customer analytics to enhance personalized marketing and boost market share.

Practical Steps

1. **Quantify Benefits:** Use metrics such as dollar savings, time reductions, or customer satisfaction scores to measure potential impact.
2. **Engage Stakeholders:** Collaborate with business units to understand the direct and indirect benefits of the initiative.
3. **Model Scenarios:** Simulate outcomes to estimate how the project will influence key performance indicators (KPIs).

---

2. Assessing Feasibility

Even high-impact projects can falter if they are overly complex or resource-intensive. Evaluating feasibility ensures that chosen initiatives are practical and achievable within organizational constraints.

Key Considerations

- **Technical Complexity:**
  Assess the level of expertise, integration requirements, and technology upgrades needed.
    - **Example:** Projects requiring significant changes to legacy code may face higher technical barriers.
- **Resource Requirements:**
  Evaluate the time, budget, and personnel needed to

complete the initiative.

  - **Example:** Training ML models may demand substantial computational power and skilled data scientists.

- **Risk Factors:**
  Identify potential obstacles, such as implementation challenges, system downtime risks, or regulatory compliance issues.
  - **Example:** Real-time fraud detection models must comply with strict data privacy laws.

Practical Steps

1. **Resource Mapping:** Create an inventory of available resources, including hardware, software, and expertise.
2. **Risk Assessment:** Identify and plan for potential challenges, using tools like SWOT analysis (Strengths, Weaknesses, Opportunities, Threats).
3. **Pilot Testing:** Start with small-scale implementations to validate feasibility before committing to full-scale rollouts.

---

3. Creating a Prioritization Framework

A prioritization framework provides a structured way to rank projects based on their potential impact and feasibility. This ensures that resources are directed toward initiatives that offer the best return on investment.

Impact-to-Effort Ratio

This widely used approach evaluates projects by dividing their expected impact by the effort required to complete them.

- **High Impact, Low Effort:** Prioritize these for quick wins.

- **High Impact, High Effort:** Plan strategically, as these can deliver significant value over the long term.
- **Low Impact, Low Effort:** Consider these only if resources are available.
- **Low Impact, High Effort:** Avoid or defer these initiatives.

Scoring and Ranking

- **Assign Scores:** Rate each project on a scale (e.g., 1 to 5) for both impact and feasibility.
- **Calculate Total Scores:** Combine impact and feasibility scores to rank projects in order of priority.
- **Adjust for Strategic Goals:** Incorporate additional factors, such as alignment with long-term objectives or external market pressures.

Example Framework

Project	Impact (1–5)	Feasibility (1–5)	Total Score	Priority
Predictive Maintenance	5	4	9	High
Fraud Detection	4	3	7	Medium
Customer Analytics	3	5	8	High
Real-Time Optimization	5	2	7	Medium

4. Achieving Quick Wins

Quick wins are high-impact, low-complexity projects that deliver visible results in a short timeframe. These are critical for building momentum and gaining stakeholder confidence.

- **Example:** Deploying AI-based anomaly detection to monitor transaction logs, which can be implemented quickly and provides immediate security benefits.

---

5. Balancing Short-Term and Long-Term Goals

While quick wins provide immediate value, long-term strategic projects should not be overlooked. Balance your portfolio to include both types of initiatives, ensuring sustained progress.

- **Short-Term:** Projects with immediate cost savings or performance improvements.
- **Long-Term:** Complex initiatives, such as full-scale AI-driven workload optimization, which require significant investment but offer transformative benefits.

Conclusion

Prioritizing AI/ML projects based on impact and feasibility ensures that your organization focuses on initiatives that deliver the highest value with the least risk. By leveraging a structured framework, organizations can optimize resource allocation, achieve quick wins, and build a solid foundation for long-term modernization.

In the next section, we'll explore **Creating a Strategic Roadmap**, translating prioritized projects into actionable phases that ensure a smooth and effective transition to AI/ML-enabled operations.

10. Creating a Strategic Roadmap

Modernizing a mainframe environment for AI/ML integration is a complex journey that requires careful planning and execution. A strategic roadmap provides a clear path forward, breaking down the process into actionable steps and aligning efforts with organizational goals. This roadmap serves as a guiding document that keeps teams focused, minimizes risks, and ensures steady progress toward successful AI/ML adoption.

In this chapter, we will explore how to create a roadmap that balances ambition with practicality, focusing on two key aspects: structuring modernization into manageable phases and establishing measurable milestones with realistic timelines. By following these steps, organizations can navigate the intricacies of AI/ML integration with confidence and clarity.

Overview of Subtopics

1. Breaking Down Modernization into Manageable Phases

Modernization can feel overwhelming when viewed as a single, large-scale initiative. Dividing it into smaller, manageable phases makes the process more approachable and achievable. This subtopic will address:

- **How to Segment the Journey:** Identifying logical phases, such as assessment, preparation, implementation, and optimization, to streamline the process.
- **Phase-Specific Objectives:** Defining clear goals for each phase to maintain focus and measure success.

- **Building Incremental Value:** Ensuring that each phase delivers tangible outcomes that contribute to the overall modernization effort.

By breaking the journey into phases, organizations can prioritize effectively, adapt to challenges, and build momentum toward long-term transformation.

2. Setting Measurable Milestones and Timelines

A roadmap without milestones and timelines is like a ship without a compass. This subtopic will focus on how to:

- **Define Milestones:** Setting specific, measurable checkpoints to track progress and ensure accountability.
- **Estimate Timelines:** Allocating realistic timeframes for each phase and milestone, considering resource availability and organizational priorities.
- **Adjust for Flexibility:** Building room for unforeseen challenges or opportunities, allowing the roadmap to adapt to changing circumstances.

Clear milestones and timelines enable organizations to monitor progress, celebrate achievements, and maintain alignment across teams and stakeholders.

Why a Strategic Roadmap is Essential

Creating a strategic roadmap bridges the gap between vision and execution. It ensures that modernization efforts are:

- **Organized:** Provides a structured approach to tackling complex initiatives.
- **Focused:** Keeps teams aligned with overarching objectives

and avoids scope creep.

- **Measurable:** Facilitates tracking progress, identifying bottlenecks, and celebrating achievements.

With a well-defined roadmap, organizations can confidently move forward, knowing that every step contributes to a larger goal.

In the next section, we will dive into **Breaking Down Modernization into Manageable Phases**, exploring how to structure your roadmap for maximum efficiency and impact.

Breaking Down Modernization into Manageable Phases

Embarking on a mainframe modernization journey for AI/ML integration is a complex undertaking that can feel daunting without a structured approach. Dividing the process into manageable phases simplifies the effort, making it more achievable and measurable. Each phase serves as a building block, contributing to the overall transformation while maintaining focus and minimizing risk.

1. How to Segment the Journey

Modernization is best approached as a series of logical phases, each with distinct objectives and deliverables. These phases provide a clear path forward, allowing teams to concentrate on specific tasks without losing sight of the broader goal.

Common Modernization Phases

1. **Assessment:**
    - **Objective:** Gain a clear understanding of the current state of the mainframe environment.
    - **Activities:** Conduct system audits, identify bottlenecks, and evaluate readiness for AI/ML integration.
    - **Outcome:** A detailed report highlighting strengths, weaknesses, and opportunities for improvement.
2. **Preparation:**
    - **Objective:** Lay the groundwork for

modernization efforts.
    - **Activities:** Define goals, prioritize projects, and build a roadmap.
    - **Outcome:** A strategic plan with defined milestones and allocated resources.
3. **Implementation:**
    - **Objective:** Execute the modernization initiatives.
    - **Activities:** Integrate AI/ML tools, upgrade infrastructure, and deploy automation systems.
    - **Outcome:** Enhanced capabilities and the initial realization of modernization benefits.
4. **Optimization:**
    - **Objective:** Fine-tune systems to maximize performance and value.
    - **Activities:** Monitor system performance, retrain AI models, and address emerging challenges.
    - **Outcome:** A stable, efficient, and future-ready mainframe environment.

---

2. Phase-Specific Objectives

Clear objectives for each phase ensure focus and alignment with overall modernization goals. These objectives provide measurable targets that teams can use to evaluate progress and success.

Examples of Phase-Specific Objectives

- **Assessment Phase:**
    - Identify and quantify performance bottlenecks.
    - Map existing capabilities against AI/ML requirements.
- **Preparation Phase:**

  - Establish modernization goals aligned with business priorities.
  - Develop a phased implementation plan with realistic timelines.
- **Implementation Phase:**
  - Deploy AI/ML models for workload optimization.
  - Upgrade legacy systems to support modern tools and technologies.
- **Optimization Phase:**
  - Achieve a 20% reduction in system downtime through predictive maintenance.
  - Ensure continuous monitoring and adaptive improvement of AI/ML systems.

---

3. Building Incremental Value

Breaking down modernization into phases ensures that each step delivers tangible benefits, creating momentum and demonstrating value to stakeholders. This approach minimizes risk by enabling organizations to adjust strategies based on early results.

Delivering Value at Each Phase

- **Assessment Phase:**
  - **Value:** A comprehensive understanding of system performance and readiness builds confidence in the modernization plan.
- **Preparation Phase:**
  - **Value:** Clear goals and a structured roadmap provide direction and alignment among teams.
- **Implementation Phase:**

    - **Value:** Early wins, such as improved workload distribution or enhanced security, showcase the potential of modernization efforts.

- **Optimization Phase:**
    - **Value:** Long-term improvements in efficiency and reliability reinforce the return on investment.

Incremental Approach Benefits

- **Mitigates Risk:** Small, manageable steps reduce the likelihood of major setbacks.
- **Builds Confidence:** Regularly demonstrating value fosters stakeholder support and engagement.
- **Allows Flexibility:** Lessons learned in earlier phases can inform and improve subsequent efforts.

Practical Example

Scenario: Modernizing a Financial Institution's Mainframe

- **Assessment Phase:**
  The bank conducts an audit and discovers that transaction delays stem from legacy system inefficiencies.
- **Preparation Phase:**
  A roadmap is developed to prioritize upgrading the transaction processing system.
- **Implementation Phase:**
  AI/ML models are deployed to optimize transaction workflows, reducing processing times by 30%.
- **Optimization Phase:**
  Continuous monitoring identifies further improvements, such as reallocating resources during peak hours.

Conclusion

Breaking down modernization into manageable phases makes the process more structured, focused, and achievable. By defining clear objectives and ensuring incremental value, organizations can navigate the complexities of AI/ML integration while minimizing risks and maximizing results.

Next, we will explore **Setting Measurable Milestones and Timelines**, focusing on how to establish checkpoints and schedules to track progress and maintain momentum throughout the modernization journey.

Setting Measurable Milestones and Timelines

A roadmap is only effective when it includes clearly defined milestones and realistic timelines. Milestones provide checkpoints to assess progress, while timelines ensure that the project stays on track and resources are efficiently utilized. By setting measurable goals and incorporating flexibility, organizations can navigate the complexities of modernization with greater confidence and control.

1. Define Milestones

Milestones are critical checkpoints that mark significant achievements along the modernization journey. They provide a sense of progress and accountability, helping teams stay focused on the overall goals.

Key Characteristics of Effective Milestones

- **Specific and Measurable:**
  Each milestone should have a clear deliverable that can be objectively assessed.
  - **Example:** "Complete the integration of AI-based anomaly detection by Q2" is more specific and actionable than "Implement AI technologies."
- **Aligned with Objectives:**
  Milestones should directly contribute to the broader goals of the modernization initiative.
  - **Example:** If the objective is to reduce system downtime, a milestone might be "Deploy predictive maintenance models

to monitor critical components."

- **Time-Bound:**
  Milestones should have deadlines to ensure timely progress.
    - **Example:** "Finalize system audit report by the end of month one."

Examples of Milestones for Mainframe Modernization

1. **Assessment Phase:**
    - "Complete a performance baseline for mainframe operations."
    - "Identify top three system bottlenecks affecting transaction speeds."
2. **Preparation Phase:**
    - "Finalize AI/ML integration roadmap with defined phases."
    - "Secure funding and allocate resources for the implementation phase."
3. **Implementation Phase:**
    - "Deploy machine learning models for workload optimization in critical systems."
    - "Integrate AI-powered security protocols to monitor network traffic."
4. **Optimization Phase:**
    - "Reduce average transaction latency by 20% through resource reallocation."
    - "Establish a continuous monitoring framework with real-time dashboards."

---

2. Estimate Timelines

Timelines provide a structured schedule for completing each phase and milestone. Realistic timeframes are essential to avoid delays and ensure that resources are effectively managed.

Steps to Create Realistic Timelines

1. **Assess Resource Availability:**
   Consider the availability of personnel, budget, and infrastructure for each phase.
   - **Example:** If your organization has limited data science expertise, allocate extra time for training or hiring.
2. **Consider Dependencies:**
   Identify tasks that must be completed before others can begin.
   - **Example:** Conducting a system audit is a prerequisite for creating a modernization roadmap.
3. **Use Historical Data:**
   Leverage past project timelines to estimate durations for similar tasks.
   - **Example:** If previous system upgrades required three months, plan for a similar timeframe unless there are significant changes in scope or resources.
4. **Incorporate Buffer Time:**
   Build in additional time to account for unexpected delays or challenges.

Sample Timeline for a Modernization Initiative

Phase	Task	Timeframe
Assessment	Conduct system audit	4 weeks
	Analyze audit findings	2 weeks
Preparation	Develop modernization roadmap	3 weeks
	Secure funding and resources	2 weeks
Implementation	Deploy AI/ML tools	8 weeks
	Train staff on AI/ML systems	4 weeks
Optimization	Monitor and refine AI/ML models	Ongoing (monthly)

3. Adjust for Flexibility

Even the best-planned timelines can encounter unexpected changes. Flexibility is essential to adapt to challenges or take advantage of new opportunities without derailing the entire project.

Strategies for Building Flexibility

- **Establish Contingency Plans:**
  Develop backup strategies for critical tasks to minimize disruptions.
    - **Example:** If a planned software upgrade is delayed, redirect resources to other modernization tasks in the interim.
- **Allow Iterative Adjustments:**
  Use agile principles to revisit and refine milestones and timelines as new insights emerge.
    - **Example:** If initial results from AI-based workload optimization are better than expected, prioritize scaling the implementation across additional systems.
- **Track and Communicate Progress:**
  Regular progress reviews allow teams to identify potential

delays early and adjust timelines accordingly.

- **Example:** Weekly status meetings can highlight any resource bottlenecks or technical challenges.

Benefits of Clear Milestones and Timelines

Setting well-defined milestones and realistic timelines offers several advantages:

- **Accountability:** Ensures that teams remain focused on delivering specific outcomes within a set timeframe.
- **Progress Monitoring:** Enables leaders to track achievements and identify areas needing intervention.
- **Resource Efficiency:** Prevents overcommitment of resources by providing a clear schedule for their allocation.
- **Stakeholder Confidence:** Demonstrates that the modernization effort is organized and on track, fostering trust and support.

Practical Example

Scenario: Retail Organization Modernizing for AI-Driven Personalization

- **Milestone:** "Deploy recommendation engine by Q4."
- **Timeline:** Allocate six weeks for model development, three weeks for testing, and two weeks for integration.
- **Flexibility Plan:** Include a two-week buffer in case of delays during testing or data preparation.
- **Outcome:** The recommendation engine launches on time, boosting customer satisfaction and increasing sales during

the holiday season.

Conclusion

Setting measurable milestones and timelines transforms a modernization roadmap into a practical, actionable plan. By defining clear checkpoints, estimating realistic schedules, and allowing room for flexibility, organizations can ensure that their AI/ML initiatives remain focused, efficient, and adaptable.

Part IV: Data Preparation for AI/ML Integration

Data is the cornerstone of AI/ML integration. Without accurate, well-structured, and secure data, even the most advanced AI/ML models cannot deliver meaningful insights or drive effective decision-making. For organizations leveraging mainframe environments, preparing data for AI/ML integration requires addressing the unique challenges of legacy systems, vast datasets, and stringent compliance requirements.

In this part, we will explore the essential steps for ensuring your data is ready to power AI/ML initiatives. From understanding the nature of mainframe data to ensuring its security and quality, each chapter will guide you through the critical aspects of data preparation. By the end, you'll have a clear roadmap for transforming raw data into actionable intelligence, laying the foundation for successful AI/ML adoption.

Why Data Preparation Matters

AI/ML systems thrive on data, but the quality and accessibility of that data determine their effectiveness. Poorly prepared data can lead to:

- **Inaccurate Models:** Misleading predictions and unreliable insights.
- **Operational Inefficiencies:** Increased time and costs spent on troubleshooting and reprocessing.
- **Compliance Risks:** Exposure to legal and reputational challenges due to insecure or non-compliant data handling.

Conversely, well-prepared data ensures:

- **Accurate Insights:** Models trained on clean, relevant data deliver precise predictions.
- **Efficiency Gains:** Streamlined data pipelines reduce the time and resources required for analysis.
- **Regulatory Confidence:** Proper handling of sensitive data minimizes compliance risks.

Key Themes in Data Preparation

In this part, we will focus on four major themes critical to data preparation for AI/ML in mainframe environments:

1. **Understanding Mainframe Data:**
   Mainframe systems store vast amounts of business-critical data, often in formats and structures unfamiliar to modern data science practices. We'll explore how to decode and work with this data effectively.
2. **Data Extraction and Transformation:**
   Extracting data from mainframes and transforming it into formats suitable for AI/ML models can be complex. This section will provide practical techniques for efficient and accurate data processing.
3. **Ensuring Data Security and Compliance:**
   Handling sensitive data requires a deep understanding of security best practices and regulatory requirements. We'll discuss strategies to safeguard data throughout the preparation process.
4. **Addressing Data Quality Issues:**
   High-quality data is essential for effective AI/ML integration. This section will focus on identifying and

resolving inconsistencies, gaps, and other quality concerns in your datasets.

The Role of Data in AI/ML Integration

Mainframe data is a goldmine of historical and transactional information. When properly prepared, this data can:

- Power predictive analytics and decision-making models.
- Enhance customer insights and operational efficiency.
- Drive innovations that deliver competitive advantages.

By focusing on data preparation, you not only ensure the success of your AI/ML initiatives but also unlock the full potential of your mainframe systems.

Looking Ahead

In the following chapters, we'll delve deeper into each aspect of data preparation, starting with **Understanding Mainframe Data.** By understanding the characteristics and nuances of your mainframe data, you'll lay the groundwork for a seamless transition to AI/ML-enabled operations.

11. Understanding Mainframe Data

Mainframe environments have been the backbone of enterprise operations for decades, managing massive amounts of critical data. However, the nature of mainframe data is distinct, often presenting challenges when integrating with modern AI/ML workflows. Understanding the characteristics of this data and recognizing its significance in AI/ML applications are crucial steps in preparing for successful integration.

This chapter explores the foundational knowledge required to work with mainframe data, addressing its unique attributes and the importance of effective preparation. By grasping these concepts, you'll be better equipped to transform raw data into valuable insights and power AI/ML initiatives with confidence.

Overview of Subtopics

1. Characteristics of Mainframe Data

Mainframe data is unlike the structured, cloud-native datasets often used in AI/ML applications. It possesses unique attributes that can pose challenges during extraction, transformation, and integration.

We'll discuss:

- **Format Complexity:** Legacy formats like EBCDIC, VSAM, and flat files, which require specialized tools for processing.
- **Volume and Velocity:** How the immense scale of mainframe data demands robust storage and processing capabilities.

- **Transactional Nature:** The real-time, mission-critical nature of mainframe data and its implications for AI/ML use cases.
  Understanding these characteristics will provide insight into the technical and logistical requirements of preparing mainframe data for AI/ML models.

---

2. Why Data Preparation is Critical for AI/ML Success

Data preparation is the cornerstone of any AI/ML initiative. Without clean, well-structured data, even the most sophisticated models will struggle to deliver accurate and actionable insights. This subtopic will cover:

- **Data Quality Impact:** How inconsistencies, biases, or errors in data can undermine model performance.
- **Relevance to AI/ML:** Why structured, normalized, and contextually meaningful data is essential for training and deploying effective AI/ML models.
- **Challenges in Mainframe Data Preparation:** The unique obstacles associated with legacy systems and how they can be addressed.

By understanding the critical role of data preparation, you'll see how investing in these efforts ensures the success and scalability of your AI/ML projects.

Why This Chapter Matters

AI/ML success starts with the data, and mainframe environments present both opportunities and challenges in this regard. By understanding the nature of mainframe data and recognizing the importance of its preparation, you'll set the stage for a seamless and efficient transition to AI/ML-powered operations.

Next, we'll dive into **Characteristics of Mainframe Data**, exploring its complexities and implications for modern data science workflows.

Characteristics of Mainframe Data

Mainframe data is at the heart of enterprise operations, storing decades of critical information across industries such as finance, healthcare, and retail. However, its unique attributes set it apart from the structured, cloud-native datasets typically used in AI/ML applications. These characteristics present both challenges and opportunities when preparing data for AI/ML integration. Let's explore these attributes in detail.

1. Format Complexity

Mainframe systems often utilize legacy formats that require specialized tools and expertise to process. These formats can pose significant challenges for integration with modern AI/ML workflows.

Common Mainframe Data Formats

- **EBCDIC (Extended Binary Coded Decimal Interchange Code):**
  Unlike the more common ASCII format, EBCDIC is used in mainframes for encoding textual data. This requires conversion tools to make the data readable by modern systems.
    - **Challenge:** Incompatibility with AI/ML tools that rely on ASCII-based encoding.
    - **Solution:** Use specialized conversion utilities to transform EBCDIC data into standardized formats.
- **VSAM (Virtual Storage Access Method):**
  A file storage system designed for high-performance

mainframe environments. VSAM files are hierarchical and optimized for transaction processing.

  - **Challenge:** Complex structure with varying record formats.
  - **Solution:** Employ ETL (Extract, Transform, Load) tools tailored for VSAM data extraction.

- **Flat Files:**
  Simple, line-delimited files often used for batch processing. These may lack metadata, making it difficult to interpret their contents.
  - **Challenge:** Absence of descriptive headers or schema.
  - **Solution:** Collaborate with mainframe teams to decode and document the data structure.

---

2. Volume and Velocity

Mainframe environments are known for handling immense volumes of data at high speeds, making scalability a critical consideration for AI/ML integration.

Key Characteristics

- **Volume:**
  Mainframes process and store vast datasets, including decades of transactional records.
  - **Implication for AI/ML:** Training models on such large datasets requires substantial computational resources and efficient storage solutions.
- **Velocity:**
  Mainframe systems handle real-time transactions at high throughput, processing thousands of records per second.
  - **Implication for AI/ML:** Real-time data pipelines and streaming analytics are essential to maintain operational

efficiency.

Best Practices

- **Leverage Scalable Infrastructure:** Use distributed computing platforms like Hadoop or Spark for processing large datasets.
- **Batch vs. Streaming:** Implement hybrid solutions that balance batch processing for historical data with streaming for real-time analysis.

---

3. Transactional Nature

Mainframe data is highly transactional, supporting mission-critical applications that demand precision and reliability.

Characteristics of Transactional Data

- **Real-Time Accuracy:**
  Mainframes often manage systems such as banking transactions, airline reservations, and healthcare records, where even minor delays or inaccuracies can have significant consequences.
  - **Implication for AI/ML:** Models must be robust enough to operate in real-time without compromising accuracy.
- **Complex Interdependencies:**
  Many transactions involve interdependent records that must be updated consistently.
  - **Implication for AI/ML:** Ensuring data consistency is vital when extracting and integrating datasets for analysis.

Use Cases

- **Fraud Detection:** Real-time monitoring of transactional data for unusual patterns.
- **Predictive Maintenance:** Using log data to identify potential failures before they disrupt operations.

Implications for AI/ML Integration

The unique characteristics of mainframe data demand specialized strategies for AI/ML integration:

- **Preprocessing Requirements:** Legacy formats must be converted and structured for modern AI/ML workflows.
- **Scalability Challenges:** Large volumes of data necessitate robust storage and processing capabilities.
- **Real-Time Capabilities:** AI/ML models must integrate seamlessly with the transactional nature of mainframe operations.

By understanding these attributes, organizations can better prepare their mainframe data for AI/ML applications, ensuring that they leverage the full potential of their systems.

Conclusion

Mainframe data is a powerful asset for enterprises, but its complexity, scale, and transactional nature require tailored approaches for AI/ML integration. In the next section, we will explore **Why Data Preparation is Critical for AI/ML Success**, examining the foundational steps necessary to transform raw mainframe data into actionable intelligence.

Why Data Preparation is Critical for AI/ML Success

Data preparation is the bedrock of any AI/ML initiative, especially in environments as complex as mainframes. No matter how advanced the algorithms or powerful the computational infrastructure, the quality and structure of the input data ultimately dictate the success of the model. Data preparation ensures that raw data is transformed into a form that is clean, structured, and meaningful, allowing AI/ML systems to perform optimally and deliver actionable insights.

1. Data Quality Impact

Poor-quality data can derail even the most sophisticated AI/ML models, leading to inaccurate predictions, unreliable results, and costly errors.

How Data Quality Affects Model Performance

- **Inconsistencies:**
  Inconsistent data, such as mismatched formats or duplicate records, can confuse models and reduce accuracy.
    - **Example:** An AI fraud detection system may overlook fraudulent transactions due to inconsistent transaction records.
- **Biases:**
  Biased data leads to biased models, which can perpetuate systemic inequities or produce skewed results.
    - **Example:** A biased loan approval model trained on historical data may unfairly reject certain demographic

groups.

- **Errors:**
  Missing or incorrect values can severely limit the model's ability to learn meaningful patterns.
    - **Example:** Gaps in customer data might hinder predictive analytics for churn reduction.

Mitigating Data Quality Issues

1. **Data Cleaning:** Remove or correct inaccuracies, duplicates, and irrelevant records.
2. **Normalization:** Standardize data formats to ensure uniformity.
3. **Validation:** Implement processes to verify the accuracy and completeness of datasets.

---

2. Relevance to AI/ML

AI/ML models require data that is not only clean but also structured and contextually meaningful. Properly prepared data ensures that models can extract the patterns and relationships needed to perform their tasks effectively.

Why Structured Data Matters

- **Improved Model Training:** Structured and normalized data allows models to learn efficiently without being distracted by irrelevant noise.
    - **Example:** Normalizing transaction timestamps ensures consistency when analyzing seasonal trends.
- **Contextual Relevance:** Data must be meaningful within the context of the problem being addressed.
    - **Example:** For workload optimization on mainframes, data

on CPU usage and job scheduling is more relevant than unrelated system logs.

Steps for Structuring Data

1. **Feature Engineering:** Extract and create features that are most relevant to the AI/ML task.
2. **Categorization:** Organize data into meaningful groups or labels for classification tasks.
3. **Contextual Annotation:** Add metadata or descriptions to enhance the interpretability of the data.

---

3. Challenges in Mainframe Data Preparation

Mainframe environments pose unique challenges that make data preparation particularly complex. These obstacles stem from the legacy nature of the systems and the scale at which they operate.

Unique Obstacles

- **Legacy Data Formats:** Mainframes often store data in formats like EBCDIC or VSAM, which are incompatible with modern AI/ML tools.
  - **Solution:** Use ETL (Extract, Transform, Load) processes to convert data into AI/ML-compatible formats.
- **Large Volumes of Data:** Mainframes process and store massive datasets, making data extraction and transformation resource-intensive.
  - **Solution:** Implement scalable data pipelines that can handle batch and real-time processing.
- **Data Silos:** Data is often fragmented across systems, creating barriers to integration.
  - **Solution:** Leverage data integration tools to consolidate

information into unified datasets.

- **Compliance Requirements:** Strict regulatory standards may limit how data can be accessed, stored, and processed.
    - **Solution:** Work with legal and compliance teams to establish secure and compliant data pipelines.

Addressing the Challenges

1. **Invest in Specialized Tools:** Use mainframe-specific ETL tools and middleware for seamless data processing.
2. **Collaborate Across Teams:** Engage mainframe administrators, data scientists, and compliance officers to ensure holistic preparation.
3. **Adopt Agile Methods:** Use iterative approaches to test and refine data preparation strategies.

Why Invest in Data Preparation?

Data preparation is not just a prerequisite—it's an investment in the long-term success of AI/ML projects. By dedicating time and resources to cleaning, structuring, and contextualizing data, organizations can:

- **Improve Model Accuracy:** High-quality data results in more reliable predictions and insights.
- **Enhance Efficiency:** Streamlined data pipelines reduce processing times and resource usage.
- **Mitigate Risks:** Compliant and well-managed data minimizes legal and operational vulnerabilities.

Conclusion

Effective data preparation ensures that AI/ML models are built on a strong foundation, maximizing their potential to deliver actionable insights and drive enterprise innovation. In the next section, we will explore the **Tools and Techniques for Extracting and Transforming Data**, providing practical strategies for handling mainframe data at scale.

12. Data Extraction and Transformation

Data extraction and transformation are critical steps in preparing mainframe data for AI/ML integration. The goal is to extract relevant data from mainframe systems, transform it into formats compatible with modern tools, and ensure that it is clean, structured, and ready for analysis. These processes form the backbone of data preparation, enabling organizations to unlock the full potential of their mainframe environments in AI/ML applications.

In this chapter, we'll explore the core processes and methodologies required for effective data extraction and transformation. From understanding the intricacies of ETL (Extract, Transform, Load) workflows to leveraging specialized tools, this chapter will provide you with actionable insights to streamline your data preparation efforts.

Overview of Subtopics

1. ETL (Extract, Transform, Load) Processes for Mainframe Data

The ETL process is fundamental to handling mainframe data, involving:

- **Extraction:** Retrieving raw data from mainframe systems while maintaining its integrity.
- **Transformation:** Converting, cleaning, and structuring data to meet the requirements of AI/ML models.

- **Loading:** Transferring the processed data into a target system, such as a data warehouse or analytics platform. This subtopic will detail the challenges and best practices for each stage, focusing on the unique complexities of working with mainframe environments.

---

2. Tools and Techniques for Data Transformation

Data transformation involves converting raw, unstructured, or incompatible data into a format suitable for analysis and modeling. This subtopic will cover:

- **Specialized Tools:** An overview of software and platforms tailored for mainframe data transformation, such as Informatica, Talend, and IBM DataStage.
- **Transformation Techniques:** Methods like normalization, feature engineering, and format conversion to ensure data is optimized for AI/ML tasks.
- **Scalability and Automation:** Strategies to handle large datasets efficiently and automate repetitive processes. We'll explore how these tools and techniques can help bridge the gap between legacy systems and modern data science workflows.

Why This Chapter Matters

Data extraction and transformation are pivotal to AI/ML success. Without these processes, raw mainframe data remains inaccessible and unusable for modern analytical methods. Mastering these concepts ensures that your organization can:

- Seamlessly integrate mainframe data into AI/ML pipelines.
- Enhance data quality and consistency for accurate modeling.
- Streamline operations by automating time-intensive tasks.

Looking Ahead

In the next sections, we will dive deeper into **ETL Processes for Mainframe Data**, exploring how to extract, transform, and load data efficiently while overcoming common challenges. By mastering these techniques, you'll be better equipped to prepare your data for AI/ML integration and unlock its full potential.

ETL (Extract, Transform, Load) Processes for Mainframe Data

The ETL (Extract, Transform, Load) process is a critical workflow for preparing mainframe data for AI/ML integration. It enables organizations to extract raw data from legacy systems, transform it into actionable formats, and load it into modern platforms for analysis and modeling. This process, while straightforward in concept, involves unique challenges and requires specialized strategies to handle the complexities of mainframe environments.

Let's examine each stage of the ETL process in detail, along with the associated challenges and best practices.

1. Extraction: Retrieving Data from Mainframes

Extraction is the first step in the ETL process, where raw data is retrieved from mainframe systems. The goal is to access the data while preserving its integrity and ensuring minimal disruption to operational systems.

Challenges

- **Legacy Formats:** Mainframe data is often stored in formats like EBCDIC, VSAM, or IMS databases, which are incompatible with modern tools.
- **Real-Time Access:** Retrieving data from live systems without impacting performance can be challenging, especially in high-demand environments.
- **Data Silos:** Mainframe environments may have

fragmented data across different systems and applications.

Best Practices

1. **Use Specialized Extraction Tools:** Employ tools like IBM DataStage, Informatica, or custom scripts designed for mainframe systems to handle complex formats and ensure efficient extraction.
2. **Leverage Incremental Extraction:** Instead of retrieving the entire dataset, extract only new or updated data to reduce resource usage and processing time.
3. **Maintain Data Integrity:** Implement validation checks to ensure that the extracted data is complete and accurate.

---

2. Transformation: Converting, Cleaning, and Structuring Data

The transformation stage involves converting raw data into a format suitable for AI/ML models. This includes cleaning the data to remove inconsistencies, normalizing it for uniformity, and structuring it to meet analytical requirements.

Challenges

- **Data Quality Issues:** Legacy systems may contain incomplete, inconsistent, or duplicate records that need cleaning.
- **Format Conversion:** Data from mainframes often needs to be converted from proprietary formats (e.g., EBCDIC to ASCII) or structured into relational schemas.
- **Feature Engineering:** Preparing data for AI/ML involves creating features that enhance the model's learning capabilities.

Best Practices

1. **Automate Data Cleaning:** Use tools like Talend or Python libraries such as Pandas to automate cleaning tasks like deduplication, normalization, and outlier detection.
2. **Standardize Formats:** Convert legacy formats into standardized, AI/ML-compatible formats such as CSV, JSON, or Parquet.
3. **Feature Engineering:** Extract meaningful features from raw data that align with AI/ML objectives. For example:
    - Aggregate transaction amounts for fraud detection.
    - Derive CPU usage metrics for workload optimization.
4. **Validate Transformations:** Use sample testing to verify that transformations preserve data accuracy and context.

---

3. Loading: Moving Data into Target Systems

The final step in the ETL process is loading the transformed data into a target system, such as a data warehouse, data lake, or AI/ML pipeline. This ensures that the data is accessible for analysis and modeling.

Challenges

- **Large Data Volumes:** Mainframes generate massive datasets, which can overwhelm storage and processing systems during loading.
- **Latency Requirements:** AI/ML applications often require real-time or near-real-time data access, which complicates the loading process.

- **Integration Complexity:** Target systems must integrate seamlessly with mainframe environments.

Best Practices

1. **Optimize Loading Pipelines:** Use scalable storage solutions, such as Hadoop, Amazon S3, or Snowflake, to handle large datasets efficiently.
2. **Batch and Stream Processing:** Implement hybrid approaches that combine batch loading for historical data with streaming for real-time updates.
3. **Monitor Load Performance:** Regularly evaluate load times and optimize configurations to minimize delays.
4. **Secure Data Transfers:** Use encryption and secure protocols to protect sensitive data during loading.

Example: ETL Workflow for a Financial Institution

Scenario:

A bank needs to integrate transactional data from its mainframe systems into an AI/ML pipeline for fraud detection.

ETL Steps:

1. **Extraction:**
    - Use IBM DataStage to extract transaction logs stored in VSAM format.
    - Validate the extracted data to ensure completeness.
2. **Transformation:**
    - Convert data from EBCDIC to ASCII format for compatibility.

    - Clean and normalize transaction records to remove duplicates and fill missing values.
    - Engineer features such as transaction frequency and amount deviation.
3. **Loading:**
    - Load the transformed data into a cloud-based data lake (e.g., AWS S3) for scalability.
    - Set up a streaming pipeline for real-time transaction updates using Kafka.

Outcome:

The bank achieves real-time fraud detection with AI/ML models powered by high-quality, well-prepared data.

Conclusion

The ETL process is foundational to unlocking the value of mainframe data for AI/ML initiatives. By addressing the challenges of extraction, transformation, and loading with targeted strategies and best practices, organizations can ensure that their data is ready to drive powerful, actionable insights.

In the next section, we will explore **Tools and Techniques for Data Transformation**, focusing on the platforms and methods that simplify and optimize the transformation stage for mainframe environments.

Tools and Techniques for Data Transformation

Data transformation is a critical step in preparing mainframe data for AI/ML workflows. The process involves converting raw, unstructured, or incompatible data into formats that AI/ML models can analyze and understand. Proper transformation ensures that the data is clean, structured, and optimized for the intended use, bridging the gap between legacy mainframe systems and modern data science platforms.

Let's delve into the tools, techniques, and strategies that streamline and enhance data transformation.

1. Specialized Tools for Data Transformation

Specialized tools simplify the complex process of transforming mainframe data, offering features tailored to legacy environments and AI/ML requirements. Here are some of the most commonly used platforms:

Informatica

- **Capabilities:**
  Offers robust ETL functionalities with support for legacy data formats and integration with modern platforms like cloud data warehouses.
    - **Features:** Data masking, data cleansing, and AI/ML-based anomaly detection during transformation.
    - **Use Case:** Transforming EBCDIC data into standardized CSV for predictive maintenance models.

Talend

- **Capabilities:**
  Provides an open-source ETL platform with extensive support for data transformation tasks, including format conversion, validation, and integration.
    - **Features:** Real-time data processing, drag-and-drop interface, and support for mainframe connectors.
    - **Use Case:** Normalizing transactional data from VSAM files for fraud detection algorithms.

IBM DataStage

- **Capabilities:**
  A mainframe-native tool designed to handle large-scale data transformation processes efficiently.
    - **Features:** Parallel processing, metadata management, and built-in support for mainframe file systems.
    - **Use Case:** Preparing log data for anomaly detection in enterprise systems.

Apache Spark

- **Capabilities:**
  A distributed data processing engine ideal for handling large-scale data transformations.
    - **Features:** Scalable, in-memory processing with machine learning libraries (MLlib) for advanced data preparation.
    - **Use Case:** Batch processing of historical mainframe data for AI/ML model training.

---

2. Transformation Techniques

Transformation techniques involve applying specific methods to clean, structure, and enhance raw data. These techniques ensure the data is ready for AI/ML applications.

Normalization

- **Definition:**
  Standardizing data to eliminate inconsistencies in scale, units, or formats.
  - **Example:** Converting currency values into a single format (e.g., USD) for global financial analysis.
  - **Benefit:** Improves model accuracy by ensuring uniformity in input data.

Feature Engineering

- **Definition:**
  Creating new variables or features that enhance a model's ability to learn patterns.
  - **Example:** Deriving "average transaction amount" or "time since last login" from raw data for customer behavior analysis.
  - **Benefit:** Enables AI/ML models to capture complex relationships within the data.

Format Conversion

- **Definition:**
  Transforming data from legacy formats (e.g., EBCDIC, flat files) into modern formats like JSON, Parquet, or CSV.
  - **Example:** Converting VSAM files into a relational schema for SQL-based analytics.
  - **Benefit:** Ensures compatibility with AI/ML tools and platforms.

3. Scalability and Automation

Given the scale and complexity of mainframe data, scalability and automation are essential for efficient transformation processes.

Scalability Strategies

- **Distributed Processing:**
  Leverage platforms like Apache Spark or Hadoop to process large datasets across multiple nodes.
    - **Example:** Splitting a 10 TB dataset into chunks for parallel processing during transformation.
- **Cloud-Based Solutions:**
  Use cloud platforms like AWS Glue or Google Dataflow for elastic scaling based on workload demands.
    - **Example:** Scaling up resources during peak data processing times and scaling down during off-peak periods.

Automation Techniques

- **Reusable Pipelines:**
  Build automated ETL pipelines using tools like Talend or Informatica to handle repetitive tasks such as data cleansing and format conversion.
    - **Example:** Automating the daily transformation of transactional data into a structured database for AI/ML analysis.
- **Machine Learning for Transformation:**
  Apply ML algorithms to automate tasks like anomaly detection, pattern recognition, and data cleansing.
    - **Example:** Using ML models to identify and correct inconsistencies in customer records.

How Tools and Techniques Bridge Legacy and Modern Workflows

By leveraging specialized tools, transformation techniques, and scalable strategies, organizations can overcome the challenges of working with mainframe data:

- **Improved Data Quality:** Tools like Talend and Informatica automate data cleansing, ensuring higher accuracy and consistency.
- **Efficient Processing:** Distributed platforms like Apache Spark handle large-scale transformations, reducing processing time.
- **Seamless Integration:** Techniques like format conversion enable compatibility between mainframe data and modern AI/ML workflows.

Example: Transforming Data for AI-Powered Customer Insights

Scenario:

A retail organization uses mainframes to store customer transaction records and wants to leverage AI to generate personalized recommendations.

Steps:

1. **Extraction:**
   Use IBM DataStage to retrieve customer records from VSAM files.
2. **Transformation:**
   - Convert EBCDIC to ASCII format.

  - Normalize data by standardizing transaction timestamps.
  - Engineer features like "average transaction value" and "most frequent purchase category."
3. **Loading:**
   Load the transformed data into a cloud-based data lake (e.g., AWS S3) for AI/ML model training.

Outcome:

The organization delivers personalized recommendations, increasing customer satisfaction and sales.

Conclusion

Data transformation is a vital step in the AI/ML integration journey, ensuring that raw mainframe data is clean, structured, and ready for analysis. By using specialized tools, adopting robust techniques, and implementing scalable strategies, organizations can streamline their transformation processes and unlock the full potential of their data.

In the next section, we'll delve into **Ensuring Data Security and Compliance**, exploring strategies to safeguard sensitive data and meet regulatory requirements during data preparation.

13. Ensuring Data Security and Compliance

In the digital age, data security and compliance are non-negotiable, especially when handling sensitive and mission-critical data stored in mainframe systems. As organizations integrate AI/ML into their operations, they must prioritize safeguarding data against breaches and ensuring adherence to industry regulations. A single oversight can lead to financial penalties, reputational damage, and erosion of customer trust.

This chapter focuses on the dual imperatives of protecting sensitive data and navigating the complex landscape of compliance in regulated industries. By addressing these challenges proactively, organizations can create a secure foundation for their AI/ML initiatives.

Overview of Subtopics

1. Protecting Sensitive Data

The data stored on mainframes often includes highly confidential information such as financial transactions, healthcare records, and customer details. This subtopic will explore:

- **Threats to Data Security:** The risks posed by cyberattacks, insider threats, and misconfigurations.
- **Encryption and Access Control:** Tools and practices for securing data at rest, in transit, and during processing.
- **Data Anonymization:** Techniques to mask personally identifiable information (PII) while maintaining its

analytical value.
By implementing robust security measures, organizations can protect their most valuable assets and mitigate risks.

---

2. Compliance Considerations for Regulated Industries

Industries such as finance, healthcare, and retail operate under strict regulatory frameworks designed to safeguard customer data and ensure ethical practices. This subtopic will discuss:

- **Key Regulations:** An overview of standards like GDPR, HIPAA, and PCI DSS, and their implications for data preparation and AI/ML workflows.
- **Auditing and Reporting:** How to document compliance efforts and prepare for audits.
- **Integrating Compliance into AI/ML Pipelines:** Strategies to ensure that data handling practices align with regulatory requirements.
  Navigating compliance challenges effectively ensures that organizations avoid penalties and maintain trust with stakeholders.

Why This Chapter Matters

AI/ML integration introduces new dimensions of complexity to data security and compliance. As organizations modernize their mainframe environments, they must adapt to evolving threats and regulations. Failing to address these concerns can derail even the most promising initiatives, while proactive measures pave the way for secure and scalable innovation.

Looking Ahead

In the following sections, we'll dive deeper into **Protecting Sensitive Data**, examining the tools and techniques that safeguard critical information in mainframe environments. By understanding the foundational principles of security and compliance, you'll be equipped to build robust systems that support your organization's AI/ML goals without compromising on safety or integrity.

Protecting Sensitive Data

Mainframes have long been trusted to store and process the most sensitive and mission-critical data for industries such as finance, healthcare, and government. However, as these systems integrate with modern AI/ML workflows, they become part of an expanded attack surface, facing both traditional and emerging threats. Protecting sensitive data is paramount to maintaining operational integrity, ensuring compliance, and safeguarding customer trust.

1. Threats to Data Security

Mainframe data is a high-value target for malicious actors, and understanding potential threats is the first step toward safeguarding it.

Key Threats

- **Cyberattacks:**
    - **External Threats:** Hackers and ransomware groups target mainframes due to the wealth of sensitive data they store.
    - **Mitigation:** Implement firewalls, intrusion detection systems (IDS), and regular penetration testing.
- **Insider Threats:**
    - **Definition:** Employees or contractors who misuse their access to data for malicious or negligent purposes.
    - **Mitigation:** Apply role-based access controls (RBAC) and monitor user activity to identify anomalies.
- **Misconfigurations:**
    - **Definition:** Poorly configured systems can unintentionally

expose sensitive data, increasing the risk of breaches.
  - **Mitigation:** Conduct routine configuration reviews and implement automated compliance checks.

Best Practices for Threat Mitigation

1. **Regular Audits:** Conduct periodic security audits to identify vulnerabilities.
2. **Monitoring and Alerts:** Use tools to detect and respond to suspicious activity in real-time.
3. **Incident Response Plans:** Develop clear protocols for responding to data breaches and minimizing their impact.

---

2. Encryption and Access Control

Encryption and access control are two critical layers of defense that ensure sensitive data remains secure, even if accessed by unauthorized parties.

Encryption

- **Data at Rest:**
  Encrypt data stored on mainframes using strong encryption algorithms like AES-256. This ensures that even if storage devices are compromised, the data remains inaccessible without the decryption key.
  - **Example:** Encrypting customer credit card data in a financial database.
- **Data in Transit:**
  Use secure protocols such as TLS (Transport Layer Security) to encrypt data as it moves between systems, reducing the risk of interception during transmission.

    - **Example:** Protecting transaction logs sent from a mainframe to a cloud-based data warehouse.

Access Control

- **Role-Based Access Control (RBAC):**
  Assign access permissions based on job roles, ensuring employees can only access the data necessary for their tasks.
    - **Example:** Allowing database administrators to manage records without accessing sensitive financial data.
- **Multi-Factor Authentication (MFA):**
  Add an extra layer of security by requiring users to verify their identity through multiple factors, such as a password and a smartphone app.
    - **Example:** Requiring MFA for all mainframe operators accessing sensitive systems.

Best Practices for Encryption and Access Control

1. **Key Management:** Securely manage encryption keys using tools like hardware security modules (HSMs).
2. **Periodic Reviews:** Regularly review and update access permissions to align with changing roles and responsibilities.
3. **End-to-End Encryption:** Ensure encryption is maintained throughout the entire data lifecycle.

---

3. Data Anonymization

Data anonymization ensures that sensitive information is protected while maintaining its usability for AI/ML applications.

Techniques for Anonymization

- **Masking:** Replace sensitive information with placeholder characters or hashed values to obscure it.
    - **Example:** Replacing a customer's name with a random identifier in training datasets.
- **Tokenization:** Substitute sensitive data with non-sensitive tokens that can be mapped back to the original values if needed.
    - **Example:** Replacing credit card numbers with unique tokens in transaction records.
- **Aggregation:** Combine data points to present summarized insights rather than individual details.
    - **Example:** Reporting average customer spending per region instead of individual purchase histories.

Benefits of Anonymization

- **Compliance:** Meet regulatory requirements such as GDPR or HIPAA by reducing the risks associated with PII.
- **Data Utility:** Retain analytical value for AI/ML tasks while eliminating the exposure of sensitive information.

Best Practices for Data Anonymization

1. **Consistent Policies:** Apply anonymization standards uniformly across datasets to maintain consistency.
2. **Reversible Methods with Care:** Use reversible anonymization methods (e.g., tokenization) only when strictly necessary, and protect mapping data.
3. **Testing and Validation:** Regularly test anonymized

datasets to ensure they still meet AI/ML requirements.

Conclusion

Protecting sensitive data is a critical responsibility in AI/ML workflows, particularly in mainframe environments that handle vast amounts of confidential information. By understanding the threats, implementing robust encryption and access control measures, and adopting effective anonymization techniques, organizations can mitigate risks and create a secure foundation for their AI/ML initiatives.

In the next section, we will explore **Compliance Considerations for Regulated Industries**, examining how organizations can navigate regulatory requirements to ensure their data practices align with legal and ethical standards.

Compliance Considerations for Regulated Industries

In industries such as finance, healthcare, and retail, where data is both a critical asset and a sensitive liability, compliance with regulatory frameworks is essential. These regulations are designed to protect customer data, promote ethical practices, and ensure accountability. Integrating AI/ML into mainframe environments requires organizations to navigate these compliance challenges carefully, ensuring that data handling practices align with legal standards while enabling innovation.

1. Key Regulations

Understanding the most significant regulatory frameworks is essential for building compliant AI/ML workflows. Here's an overview of key regulations and their implications:

GDPR (General Data Protection Regulation)

- **Scope:** Governs the processing of personal data for EU residents, regardless of where the organization is based.
- **Key Requirements:**
    - Data minimization: Only collect data that is strictly necessary.
    - Explicit consent: Obtain clear permission for data usage.
    - Data portability: Allow individuals to access and transfer their data.
- **AI/ML Implications:**
    - Models must ensure transparency in how personal

data is used and allow individuals to opt out of automated decision-making processes.

HIPAA (Health Insurance Portability and Accountability Act)

- **Scope:** Protects the privacy and security of healthcare information in the U.S.
- **Key Requirements:**
    - Safeguards for electronic protected health information (ePHI).
    - Limitations on data sharing without patient consent.
- **AI/ML Implications:**
    - Data used for AI/ML in healthcare must be anonymized or de-identified to comply with HIPAA rules while still enabling valuable analytics.

PCI DSS (Payment Card Industry Data Security Standard)

- **Scope:** Ensures secure handling of payment card information globally.
- **Key Requirements:**
    - Encryption of cardholder data at rest and in transit.
    - Regular vulnerability scans and penetration tests.
- **AI/ML Implications:**
    - Data used for fraud detection models must adhere to encryption and masking requirements to prevent unauthorized access.

---

2. Auditing and Reporting

Compliance isn't just about adhering to regulations; it's also about demonstrating that adherence. Auditing and reporting are crucial for proving compliance to regulators and stakeholders.

Auditing Practices

- **Periodic Audits:** Regularly review data handling practices to identify gaps and ensure ongoing compliance.
- **Audit Trails:** Maintain logs of data access, processing, and storage to document accountability.
- **Third-Party Assessments:** Engage independent auditors to validate compliance efforts and identify risks.

Reporting Requirements

- **Compliance Reports:** Generate detailed reports that outline compliance measures, including data handling policies, security controls, and incident response plans.
- **Incident Reporting:** Develop protocols to report data breaches or security incidents promptly to regulatory authorities, as required by regulations like GDPR and HIPAA.
- **Stakeholder Communication:** Provide transparent updates to customers and partners about compliance efforts and data protection practices.

Best Practices for Auditing and Reporting

1. **Automate Auditing Tools:** Use platforms that automatically monitor and log compliance activities.
2. **Conduct Mock Audits:** Simulate audit scenarios to test readiness and identify gaps.
3. **Create a Centralized Repository:** Maintain all

compliance documentation in an accessible and organized format.

---

3. Integrating Compliance into AI/ML Pipelines

Compliance cannot be an afterthought in AI/ML workflows. Instead, it must be an integral part of the data pipeline to ensure that all processing activities align with regulatory requirements.

Strategies for Integration

- **Data Governance Policies:**
    - Define clear rules for data access, usage, and retention that comply with industry regulations.
    - Example: Implement role-based access controls to limit exposure to sensitive information.
- **Built-In Anonymization:**
    - Incorporate anonymization techniques, such as masking or encryption, directly into data pipelines.
    - Example: Tokenize customer identifiers before feeding data into AI/ML models.
- **Explainability and Transparency:**
    - Ensure that AI/ML models provide explanations for their decisions, particularly in regulated industries like finance and healthcare.
    - Example: Use interpretable models that allow regulators and customers to understand the logic behind automated decisions.
- **Regular Compliance Checks:**
    - Periodically validate that AI/ML workflows comply with evolving regulatory requirements.

   - Example: Implement tools that scan datasets for sensitive information and flag non-compliance.

Benefits of Compliance Integration

- **Reduced Risk:** Proactive measures minimize the likelihood of data breaches or regulatory penalties.
- **Enhanced Trust:** Demonstrating compliance builds confidence among customers, partners, and stakeholders.
- **Operational Efficiency:** Automating compliance within pipelines reduces the manual effort required to ensure adherence.

Why Compliance Matters

In a world where data is both a competitive advantage and a liability, compliance is more than a regulatory requirement—it's a business imperative. Effective compliance measures:

- Protect organizations from legal and financial penalties.
- Strengthen customer trust and loyalty by demonstrating a commitment to data protection.
- Enable innovation by creating a secure foundation for integrating AI/ML into mainframe environments.

Conclusion

Navigating the regulatory landscape is a critical step in modernizing mainframe systems with AI/ML. By understanding key regulations, maintaining robust auditing and reporting practices, and integrating compliance into data pipelines, organizations can balance innovation with responsibility.

In the next section, we'll explore **How to Build Secure and Compliant AI/ML Pipelines**, providing practical strategies to operationalize compliance while optimizing for efficiency and scalability.

14. Addressing Data Quality Issues

Data quality is the foundation of any successful AI/ML initiative. Inconsistent, incomplete, or inaccurate data can undermine even the most advanced models, leading to poor predictions, unreliable insights, and operational inefficiencies. Addressing data quality issues is particularly critical in mainframe environments, where legacy systems and high data volumes often introduce unique challenges.

This chapter focuses on identifying and resolving data inconsistencies and implementing strategies for maintaining high-quality data over time. By ensuring your data meets the necessary standards, you can maximize the performance and reliability of your AI/ML workflows.

Overview of Subtopics

1. Identifying and Fixing Data Inconsistencies

Mainframe data often originates from disparate systems and legacy applications, which can lead to inconsistencies and errors. This subtopic will explore:

- **Common Data Quality Issues:** Duplicates, missing values, outdated records, and mismatched formats.
- **Detection Methods:** Tools and techniques for identifying inconsistencies using automated validation and profiling tools.
- **Fixing Data Issues:** Practical approaches to cleaning, deduplicating, and normalizing data to prepare it for AI/

ML models.
Addressing these inconsistencies ensures that data is accurate, complete, and ready for analysis.

---

2. Strategies for Ongoing Data Maintenance

Ensuring data quality is not a one-time task but an ongoing process that requires proactive monitoring and updates. This subtopic will cover:

- **Automated Monitoring:** Implementing tools and systems to continuously monitor data quality metrics.
- **Governance Practices:** Establishing policies and procedures for data stewardship and accountability.
- **Adaptability to Change:** Preparing for evolving data sources, formats, and regulatory requirements to maintain quality over time.
By implementing these strategies, organizations can sustain high-quality data pipelines that support reliable AI/ML operations.

Why This Chapter Matters

In mainframe environments, data quality issues can compound over time, leading to significant inefficiencies and inaccuracies in AI/ML outcomes. Proactively identifying and resolving these issues ensures that your organization:

- **Optimizes Model Performance:** AI/ML systems perform better with clean, accurate data.
- **Improves Decision-Making:** High-quality data leads to

more reliable insights and outcomes.

- **Reduces Costs:** Prevents the need for costly rework or corrections due to flawed data.

Looking Ahead

In the following sections, we'll begin by examining **Identifying and Fixing Data Inconsistencies**, exploring the tools and techniques available to detect and resolve common issues. With this foundation, you'll be better equipped to ensure the integrity and reliability of your data, laying the groundwork for successful AI/ML integration.

Identifying and Fixing Data Inconsistencies

Data inconsistencies are a common challenge in mainframe environments due to the nature of legacy systems and the vast amounts of data they handle. These inconsistencies, if left unchecked, can hinder AI/ML integration by introducing inaccuracies and inefficiencies. Proactively addressing these issues ensures that data is clean, accurate, and ready for use in AI/ML models, ultimately enabling better decision-making and operational performance.

1. Common Data Quality Issues

Mainframe environments often accumulate data over decades, with records originating from disparate systems and formats. These factors contribute to several prevalent data quality issues:

Duplicates

- **Definition:** Multiple records representing the same entity (e.g., a customer or transaction) but stored differently.
- **Impact:** Leads to skewed analyses and inflated data volumes.
- **Example:** A customer might appear multiple times in a dataset due to slight variations in name or address spelling.

Missing Values

- **Definition:** Data fields left empty or incomplete due to system errors or inconsistent data entry practices.

- **Impact:** Reduces the reliability of AI/ML models, as they may lack critical variables for analysis.
- **Example:** Missing dates in transaction logs can disrupt time-series forecasting models.

Outdated Records

- **Definition:** Information that is no longer relevant or accurate due to changes over time.
- **Impact:** Misleads decision-making and analysis.
- **Example:** Old customer contact details affecting marketing efforts.

Mismatched Formats

- **Definition:** Data stored in different formats or encodings that are incompatible with modern systems.
- **Impact:** Increases processing complexity and risks data loss during integration.
- **Example:** Legacy systems storing text in EBCDIC format, which must be converted to ASCII for analysis.

---

2. Detection Methods

The first step in resolving data inconsistencies is identifying them using robust detection techniques. Automated tools and systematic approaches can simplify this process:

Automated Validation Tools

- **Tools:** Talend Data Quality, IBM Infosphere QualityStage, Informatica Data Quality.

- **Functionality:** Scan datasets to identify issues such as duplicates, null values, and anomalies in data formats.
- **Example:** A validation tool might flag duplicate customer records based on matching email addresses or phone numbers.

Data Profiling Techniques

- **Definition:** Analyzing datasets to uncover patterns, inconsistencies, and structural errors.
- **Key Metrics:** Assess completeness, uniqueness, and consistency across datasets.
- **Example:** Profiling a sales dataset to identify outliers in transaction amounts.

Rule-Based Detection

- **Definition:** Applying predefined rules to flag errors.
- **Example Rules:**
    - Flagging transactions with negative amounts.
    - Identifying records with missing primary keys (e.g., customer IDs).

AI-Powered Solutions

- **Tools:** AI/ML algorithms designed to identify patterns and anomalies in large datasets.
- **Example:** Using machine learning to detect suspicious patterns indicative of duplicates or errors.

---

3. Fixing Data Issues

Once inconsistencies are identified, the next step is to resolve them through targeted cleaning, deduplication, and normalization efforts.

Data Cleaning

- **Definition:** Removing or correcting errors and inconsistencies.
- **Techniques:**
    - **Filling Missing Values:** Use imputation methods such as mean substitution, predictive algorithms, or interpolation.
    - **Removing Irrelevant Records:** Filter out outdated or irrelevant entries.
- **Example:** Replacing missing birthdates with an estimated median value for customer age segmentation.

Deduplication

- **Definition:** Consolidating multiple records representing the same entity.
- **Techniques:**
    - **Exact Match:** Identify duplicates with identical fields (e.g., identical customer IDs).
    - **Fuzzy Matching:** Use algorithms to identify near-duplicates based on probabilistic scoring (e.g., Levenshtein distance).
- **Example:** Merging customer records with similar names but matching phone numbers.

Normalization

- **Definition:** Standardizing data formats and values to ensure uniformity.
- **Techniques:**
    - Convert date formats (e.g., "MM/DD/YYYY" to

ISO format "YYYY-MM-DD").
  - Normalize text case for consistency (e.g., converting names to title case).
- **Example:** Standardizing addresses to follow a unified postal format for better geolocation analysis.

Case Study: Resolving Data Quality Issues in Financial Systems

Scenario:

A bank needs to prepare mainframe transaction data for fraud detection using AI/ML.

Steps:

1. **Identification:**
   - Used Informatica to detect duplicates in customer records and identify transactions with missing amounts.
2. **Cleaning:**
   - Imputed missing transaction amounts using average values from similar transactions.
   - Removed irrelevant entries for inactive accounts.
3. **Deduplication:**
   - Consolidated customer records based on fuzzy matching of names and addresses.
4. **Normalization:**
   - Converted all transaction timestamps to a uniform time zone.
   - Standardized currency values to USD.

Outcome:

The bank achieved a clean, high-quality dataset that significantly improved the accuracy and reliability of its fraud detection models.

Conclusion

Addressing data inconsistencies is a critical step in preparing mainframe data for AI/ML integration. By understanding common issues, leveraging detection tools, and applying effective cleaning and normalization techniques, organizations can ensure their data is accurate, reliable, and ready to drive actionable insights.

In the next section, we'll explore **Strategies for Ongoing Data Maintenance**, focusing on how to sustain data quality over time and adapt to evolving business and technological needs.

Strategies for Ongoing Data Maintenance

Maintaining data quality is not a static task but a continuous process that evolves with organizational needs, technological advancements, and regulatory changes. Without proactive strategies for ongoing maintenance, even the most robust data systems can degrade over time, jeopardizing the success of AI/ML initiatives. This section outlines key approaches to ensure the long-term integrity and usability of data pipelines in mainframe environments.

1. Automated Monitoring

Automation is a cornerstone of effective data maintenance, enabling organizations to continuously monitor and address issues before they impact operations.

Key Features of Automated Monitoring

- **Real-Time Alerts:** Automatically flag anomalies such as missing values, duplicates, or outliers as they occur.
- **Performance Dashboards:** Provide a centralized view of data quality metrics, such as completeness, accuracy, and consistency.
- **Trend Analysis:** Identify patterns over time to anticipate potential data issues.

Popular Tools for Automated Monitoring

- **Informatica Data Quality:** Offers real-time data monitoring and reporting features.

- **Talend Data Fabric:** Provides automated data profiling and issue detection.
- **IBM Infosphere:** Includes built-in capabilities for tracking data integrity across mainframe systems.

Example Implementation

A retail organization uses automated monitoring to track inconsistencies in daily sales data. An alert system notifies data stewards of missing transaction timestamps, enabling immediate correction before the data is fed into AI models for inventory predictions.

---

2. Governance Practices

Strong governance practices create a framework for accountability, ensuring data quality is managed systematically across teams and departments.

Core Components of Data Governance

- **Defined Roles and Responsibilities:**
    - Assign data stewards to oversee quality and integrity.
    - Establish escalation paths for resolving data issues.
- **Policies and Standards:**
    - Develop clear rules for data entry, processing, and validation.
    - Create documentation for standard operating procedures (SOPs).
- **Audits and Reviews:**
    - Schedule regular audits to assess adherence to governance policies.
    - Use audit findings to update and refine processes.

Example Governance Model

A healthcare provider implements a governance framework where each department designates a data steward. These stewards collaborate to enforce consistent data handling practices, ensuring compliance with HIPAA while supporting AI-driven patient care analytics.

---

3. Adaptability to Change

Data environments are dynamic, requiring strategies that adapt to new data sources, evolving formats, and shifting regulatory landscapes.

Preparing for Evolving Data Sources

- **Integration with Emerging Technologies:**
  Incorporate APIs, middleware, or cloud connectors to handle data from IoT devices, SaaS platforms, or external databases.
- **Scalable Pipelines:**
  Build flexible ETL (Extract, Transform, Load) processes that accommodate varying data volumes and formats.

Addressing Format Changes

- **Automated Format Conversion:**
  Use tools like Apache NiFi or IBM DataStage to convert legacy data formats (e.g., EBCDIC) into modern standards.
- **Versioning Systems:**
  Maintain version histories of data schemas to track changes and ensure backward compatibility.

Staying Ahead of Regulatory Shifts

- **Regulatory Monitoring:**
  Stay informed about updates to laws like GDPR, HIPAA, or PCI DSS that affect data handling requirements.
- **Built-In Compliance Checks:**
  Use tools to automatically validate data pipelines against current regulatory standards.

Example of Adaptability

A financial institution integrates data from a newly adopted mobile banking platform into its existing mainframe environment. Scalable ETL pipelines normalize and validate the new data streams, ensuring seamless integration with AI-powered fraud detection models.

Benefits of Ongoing Data Maintenance

Implementing these strategies offers several long-term advantages:

- **Sustained Data Quality:** Prevents degradation and ensures that data remains accurate, consistent, and complete.
- **Operational Efficiency:** Reduces manual intervention by automating monitoring and maintenance tasks.
- **Regulatory Compliance:** Keeps data practices aligned with evolving legal and ethical standards.
- **Scalable Growth:** Supports new technologies, business requirements, and AI/ML advancements without compromising data integrity.

Conclusion

Ongoing data maintenance is essential for building resilient, high-quality data pipelines in mainframe environments. By leveraging automated monitoring, establishing robust governance practices, and adapting to change, organizations can ensure that their data assets remain reliable and ready to power AI/ML initiatives.

Part V: Tools and Frameworks for Integration

Integrating AI/ML into mainframe environments requires the right tools and frameworks to bridge the gap between legacy systems and modern technologies. With advancements in AI/ML platforms, APIs, middleware, and hybrid cloud solutions, organizations now have access to a wide range of resources to facilitate seamless integration. However, selecting and implementing these tools effectively can be a complex task that demands a deep understanding of both mainframe systems and AI/ML workflows.

This part of the book focuses on equipping you with the knowledge to make informed decisions about tools and frameworks for integration. By exploring available options, their features, and best practices for implementation, you'll gain the insights needed to choose solutions that align with your organization's goals and constraints.

Why This Section Matters

The tools and frameworks you choose will significantly impact the success of your AI/ML initiatives. They determine how efficiently data flows between systems, how easily models can be developed and deployed, and how well your mainframe environment supports innovation. Understanding the strengths and limitations of these resources will empower you to:

- **Optimize Integration:** Reduce complexity and improve the efficiency of AI/ML workflows.
- **Enhance Scalability:** Build systems capable of handling

evolving data volumes and computational demands.

- **Drive Innovation:** Leverage advanced technologies to unlock new opportunities for growth and efficiency.

What You'll Learn

In this section, we'll explore the essential tools and frameworks that enable AI/ML integration with mainframes. From AI platforms to middleware and hybrid cloud solutions, we'll provide a comprehensive overview of their capabilities and applications. By the end of this section, you'll be equipped to:

- Identify the tools that best fit your organization's needs.
- Implement integration strategies that maximize efficiency and minimize disruption.
- Build a robust infrastructure that supports AI/ML operations while maintaining the reliability and security of your mainframe systems.

Looking Ahead

In the following chapters, we'll delve into the features, benefits, and practical applications of the tools and frameworks available for mainframe integration. We'll start by exploring an **Overview of AI/ML Tools for Mainframes**, highlighting platforms and technologies designed to bridge the gap between legacy systems and modern analytics.

15. Overview of AI/ML Tools for Mainframes

Selecting the right AI/ML tools is a pivotal step in successfully integrating advanced analytics with mainframe systems. These tools serve as the backbone of AI/ML workflows, providing the capabilities needed to build, train, deploy, and manage models effectively. With a diverse range of platforms available, from general-purpose machine learning frameworks to enterprise-grade analytics suites, understanding their features and compatibility with mainframes is essential.

This chapter provides an overview of some of the most widely used tools and platforms for AI/ML in mainframe environments. By exploring their strengths, limitations, and integration potential, you'll be better equipped to choose the tools that align with your organization's goals.

Overview of Subtopics

1. IBM Watson, TensorFlow, SAS Viya, and Others

AI/ML tools come in various forms, ranging from open-source frameworks to commercial enterprise solutions. In this section, we'll:

- Explore IBM Watson's specialized capabilities for enterprise AI, particularly in industries heavily reliant on mainframes.
- Discuss TensorFlow as a versatile open-source platform for building and training AI/ML models.
- Highlight SAS Viya's focus on advanced analytics and its

integration features tailored for enterprise-scale data operations.
- Provide insights into other tools like PyTorch, H2O.ai, and Microsoft Azure ML, which may complement or extend your existing infrastructure.

This exploration will help you understand which tools align with your specific needs, whether for flexibility, scalability, or specialized functionality.

---

2. Comparing Features and Compatibility with Mainframe Environments

Mainframe environments have unique requirements, including high reliability, scalability, and support for legacy data formats. This section will:

- Compare the capabilities of popular AI/ML tools in terms of performance, ease of use, and integration features.
- Highlight compatibility considerations, such as handling mainframe data formats, interfacing with APIs, and managing workload scalability.
- Provide practical tips for evaluating tools based on your organization's infrastructure, expertise, and objectives.

This comparison will guide you in selecting tools that not only meet technical requirements but also align with business priorities and resource availability.

Why This Chapter Matters

The tools you choose will influence every aspect of your AI/ML journey, from model development to deployment and ongoing operations. Understanding the landscape of available solutions enables you to:

- **Optimize Resource Allocation:** Invest in platforms that provide the best return on investment.
- **Enhance Integration Efficiency:** Reduce time and effort by selecting tools designed for seamless compatibility with mainframes.
- **Drive Scalability and Innovation:** Build a foundation that supports future AI/ML growth while leveraging the strengths of your mainframe environment.

Looking Ahead

In the next section, we'll take a closer look at **IBM Watson, TensorFlow, SAS Viya, and Other Tools**, diving into their key features, use cases, and potential applications in mainframe-integrated AI/ML projects. This exploration will help you identify which tools align best with your organization's unique needs and aspirations.

AI/ML Tools: IBM Watson, TensorFlow, SAS Viya, and Others

The integration of AI/ML into mainframe environments requires tools that balance advanced capabilities with compatibility and scalability. The landscape of AI/ML tools ranges from open-source frameworks offering unparalleled flexibility to enterprise-grade solutions designed for robust, large-scale operations. Here, we explore key tools that can empower your AI/ML journey and how they align with the unique demands of mainframe systems.

1. IBM Watson

IBM Watson is an enterprise-grade AI solution tailored to organizations that rely on mainframes for mission-critical operations. It provides pre-built and customizable tools for AI/ML workflows, making it a go-to choice for industries such as finance, healthcare, and logistics.

Key Features

- **Natural Language Processing (NLP):** Watson excels in understanding and generating human-like text, making it ideal for chatbots, document analysis, and automated customer support.
- **Predictive Analytics:** Tools like Watson Studio simplify the creation of predictive models by integrating seamlessly with mainframe data.
- **Integration with Mainframes:** Watson is designed to work directly with IBM Z systems, enabling smooth data

flows and real-time analytics.

Use Cases

- **Healthcare:** Deploy AI-powered diagnostic tools that analyze patient data stored on mainframes.
- **Banking:** Implement fraud detection systems by analyzing transaction patterns in real-time.

---

2. TensorFlow

TensorFlow is a leading open-source framework developed by Google, offering flexibility and power for building, training, and deploying AI/ML models. Its versatility makes it a favorite among data scientists and developers.

Key Features

- **Extensive Library Support:** TensorFlow offers a rich ecosystem of tools for deep learning, reinforcement learning, and model optimization.
- **Cross-Platform Compatibility:** Models can be deployed on multiple platforms, including edge devices, cloud systems, and on-premises mainframes.
- **Scalability:** TensorFlow supports distributed computing, making it capable of handling large datasets and complex workflows.

Use Cases

- **Retail:** Develop recommendation engines that analyze customer purchase histories stored on mainframes.

- **Telecommunications:** Predict network congestion and optimize resource allocation using historical data.

---

3. SAS Viya

SAS Viya is a comprehensive analytics platform designed for enterprise-scale data operations. Its integration capabilities and advanced analytical features make it particularly suited for mainframe environments.

Key Features

- **Visual Programming Interface:** Non-coders can use its drag-and-drop interface to create complex workflows.
- **AI/ML Integration:** Offers built-in support for machine learning models and pipelines.
- **Seamless Connectivity:** SAS Viya integrates directly with mainframe systems and supports diverse data sources, ensuring smooth interoperability.

Use Cases

- **Supply Chain Management:** Use predictive analytics to forecast demand and manage inventory.
- **Financial Services:** Analyze credit risks and market trends using mainframe-stored datasets.

---

4. Other Tools

While IBM Watson, TensorFlow, and SAS Viya are among the most prominent, other tools offer unique advantages depending on your needs:

PyTorch

- **Flexibility:** Ideal for researchers and developers who need advanced control over model design.
- **Ease of Use:** Features a dynamic computation graph that simplifies debugging and experimentation.

H2O.ai

- **AutoML Capabilities:** Simplifies model selection and hyperparameter tuning for non-expert users.
- **Speed and Scalability:** Optimized for large-scale AI/ML operations, making it suitable for mainframe data.

Microsoft Azure ML

- **Cloud Integration:** Provides robust tools for deploying AI/ML models in hybrid cloud environments.
- **Enterprise Features:** Offers pre-trained models and APIs for faster deployment.

Selecting the Right Tool for Your Organization

When evaluating AI/ML tools, consider the following:

- **Compatibility with Mainframes:** Does the tool natively support mainframe data formats and APIs?
- **Scalability:** Can it handle your organization's data volumes and computational demands?
- **Ease of Use:** Does it align with the expertise of your team, offering features like AutoML or visual programming?
- **Cost vs. Value:** Does the tool's pricing model align with

your budget and expected ROI?

Conclusion

Choosing the right AI/ML tool is a critical step in your integration journey. IBM Watson provides enterprise-grade features tailored for mainframes, TensorFlow offers unmatched flexibility, SAS Viya excels in analytics, and other tools like PyTorch, H2O.ai, and Azure ML bring additional capabilities to the table. By understanding their strengths, limitations, and use cases, you can select a toolset that aligns with your organization's goals and infrastructure.

Next, we'll delve into **Comparing Features and Compatibility with Mainframe Environments**, offering a detailed analysis of how these tools stack up and how to make an informed decision.

Comparing Features and Compatibility with Mainframe Environments

Mainframes are the backbone of critical enterprise operations, making the selection of compatible AI/ML tools essential for smooth integration. The unique demands of mainframe environments, such as reliability, scalability, and legacy data handling, necessitate careful evaluation of AI/ML tools to ensure they align with technical and business requirements.

This section explores the key considerations for selecting AI/ML tools, offering a comparison of their features, compatibility with mainframe systems, and practical tips for making informed decisions.

---

1. Comparing Capabilities of Popular AI/ML Tools

Each AI/ML tool offers unique strengths, and their suitability often depends on the specific use case and infrastructure.

Performance

- **IBM Watson:**
  Enterprise-grade performance tailored for high-stakes environments; optimized for real-time analytics and decision-making on IBM mainframes.
- **TensorFlow:**
  High computational efficiency, particularly for deep learning tasks; excels in distributed computing for large datasets.
- **SAS Viya:**

Advanced analytics with strong support for statistical and predictive modeling; designed for large-scale enterprise operations.

Ease of Use

- **IBM Watson:**
  Pre-built AI models and intuitive interfaces cater to business users as well as data scientists.
- **TensorFlow:**
  Requires technical expertise but offers flexibility for custom solutions.
- **SAS Viya:**
  Visual drag-and-drop interfaces enable non-technical users to build workflows with ease.

Integration Features

- **IBM Watson:**
  Direct integration with IBM Z systems and support for mainframe-specific APIs.
- **TensorFlow:**
  Requires middleware or custom APIs to connect with mainframe systems.
- **SAS Viya:**
  Seamlessly integrates with various mainframe and enterprise data sources.

---

2. Compatibility Considerations

Handling Mainframe Data Formats

- Mainframe data often exists in formats such as EBCDIC, VSAM, or flat files, which require specialized tools for conversion.
    - **IBM Watson:** Natively supports mainframe data formats and works with IBM DataStage for ETL tasks.
    - **TensorFlow:** Needs pre-processed data in compatible formats like CSV, JSON, or TFRecord.
    - **SAS Viya:** Directly reads and processes mainframe data formats, minimizing conversion overhead.

Interfacing with APIs

- **IBM Watson:** Pre-built APIs streamline the connection to mainframe environments and other IBM services.
- **TensorFlow:** Open-source APIs like gRPC or REST can bridge TensorFlow with mainframes, but may require custom development.
- **SAS Viya:** Offers extensive API support for seamless interaction with enterprise systems, including mainframes.

Workload Scalability

- Mainframes handle massive workloads, requiring AI/ML tools to scale without compromising performance.
    - **IBM Watson:** Designed for enterprise scalability; integrates with IBM Z hardware to leverage mainframe processing power.
    - **TensorFlow:** Supports distributed training, enabling efficient handling of large datasets across multiple nodes.
    - **SAS Viya:** Highly scalable and optimized for enterprise-grade workloads with multi-threaded processing.

---

3. Practical Tips for Evaluating Tools

When choosing AI/ML tools for mainframe integration, consider the following:

Understand Your Infrastructure

- Assess the compatibility of the tool with your existing mainframe systems, APIs, and data pipelines.
- Determine whether additional middleware or preprocessing tools are required.

Evaluate Use Case Alignment

- Match the tool's strengths to your organization's goals:
    - IBM Watson for real-time decision-making and pre-built enterprise solutions.
    - TensorFlow for flexibility in custom model development.
    - SAS Viya for user-friendly analytics and integration.

Consider Resource Availability

- Evaluate the technical expertise of your team. Tools like TensorFlow may require skilled developers, while SAS Viya and IBM Watson cater to broader user bases.
- Assess budget constraints and compare the total cost of ownership, including licensing, training, and implementation.

Case Study: Tool Selection for a Financial Institution

Scenario:

A financial institution aims to implement fraud detection using AI/ML on its IBM mainframe system.

Evaluation:

1. **IBM Watson:**
    - Direct integration with IBM Z systems simplifies implementation.
    - Pre-trained fraud detection models reduce development time.
2. **TensorFlow:**
    - Offers flexibility for custom fraud detection models but requires additional middleware for mainframe integration.
3. **SAS Viya:**
    - Provides advanced analytics for fraud detection and easily integrates with the institution's existing data pipelines.

Outcome:

The institution selects IBM Watson for its seamless compatibility with IBM Z systems, enabling rapid deployment and real-time decision-making.

Conclusion

The choice of AI/ML tools significantly influences the success of integration projects in mainframe environments. By comparing features, understanding compatibility requirements, and aligning tools with organizational needs, you can build an AI/ML ecosystem that enhances efficiency, scalability, and innovation.

In the next section, we'll explore **Using APIs and Middleware for Integration**, focusing on how these technologies facilitate seamless communication between mainframes and AI/ML tools.

16. Using APIs and Middleware for Integration

Seamless communication between mainframes and AI/ML tools is critical for successfully integrating modern analytics with legacy systems. APIs (Application Programming Interfaces) and middleware play a pivotal role in bridging this gap, enabling data to flow smoothly and ensuring compatibility between disparate technologies. These solutions allow organizations to leverage the power of AI/ML while preserving the reliability and performance of their mainframes.

This chapter explores how APIs and middleware facilitate integration, offering practical insights into selecting and implementing these technologies effectively.

Overview of Subtopics

1. Facilitating Communication Between Mainframes and AI/ML Tools

Mainframes and AI/ML tools often operate in vastly different environments, requiring a robust communication framework to enable data exchange and functional interoperability. This section will discuss:

- The role of APIs in connecting mainframes with AI/ML platforms.
- Middleware solutions that act as intermediaries, simplifying integration and reducing development complexity.

- Real-world examples of how these technologies are used in enterprise environments.

By understanding these mechanisms, you'll see how APIs and middleware enable efficient workflows and unlock the potential of AI/ML for mainframe operations.

2. Best Practices for Choosing and Implementing Middleware

Middleware acts as the glue that binds mainframes to modern technologies. Selecting and deploying the right middleware requires careful planning and consideration of both technical and organizational needs. This section will cover:

- Key criteria for evaluating middleware solutions, such as scalability, compatibility, and ease of use.
- Implementation strategies to ensure minimal disruption to existing systems.
- Tips for ongoing maintenance and updates to keep middleware running efficiently.

These best practices will empower you to choose middleware that aligns with your organization's goals while ensuring a smooth integration process.

Why This Chapter Matters

APIs and middleware are indispensable tools for creating a unified infrastructure that supports AI/ML workflows. By leveraging these technologies effectively, you can:

- **Streamline Integration:** Simplify the connection between legacy systems and modern platforms.
- **Enhance Efficiency:** Reduce the time and effort required

to move data between systems.

- **Future-Proof Your Systems:** Build a scalable foundation that supports ongoing innovation.

Looking Ahead

In the next sections, we'll delve deeper into **Facilitating Communication Between Mainframes and AI/ML Tools** and **Best Practices for Choosing and Implementing Middleware**, providing actionable insights and practical examples to help you navigate the integration process with confidence.

Facilitating Communication Between Mainframes and AI/ML Tools

Mainframes and AI/ML tools are essential components of modern enterprises, but they often operate in technologically distinct environments. Mainframes excel in reliability, security, and processing large-scale, transaction-driven workloads. Meanwhile, AI/ML tools thrive in dynamic environments where innovation and flexibility are prioritized. Bridging these differences requires robust communication frameworks to enable data exchange and functional interoperability. APIs and middleware serve as the backbone of these frameworks.

1. The Role of APIs

APIs (Application Programming Interfaces) are the primary method for enabling direct communication between systems. In mainframe-AI/ML integration, APIs act as connectors that allow different technologies to exchange information seamlessly.

How APIs Work in Integration

- **Data Retrieval:** APIs enable AI/ML tools to access mainframe data by querying datasets in real-time or batch modes.
- **Command Execution:** APIs allow AI/ML platforms to send commands to mainframes, such as initiating data transfers or triggering processes.
- **Standardization:** APIs standardize communication between systems, ensuring consistent data formats and protocols.

Types of APIs for Mainframe Integration

- **REST APIs:** Widely used for their simplicity and compatibility with modern web technologies, enabling easy access to mainframe data.
- **SOAP APIs:** Offer robust security features and reliability, often preferred in industries with strict compliance requirements like finance or healthcare.
- **Custom APIs:** Built specifically for enterprise needs, offering tailored solutions for complex mainframe-AI/ML workflows.

Example in Practice

A retail organization uses a REST API to pull customer transaction data from a mainframe into an AI/ML platform. The data is then analyzed to provide personalized product recommendations in real time.

---

2. Middleware Solutions

Middleware is software that acts as a bridge between mainframes and AI/ML tools, providing a layer of abstraction to simplify integration. Unlike APIs, middleware focuses on handling complex tasks such as data transformation, orchestration, and load balancing.

Key Functions of Middleware

- **Data Transformation:** Converts mainframe data formats (e.g., EBCDIC, VSAM) into formats compatible with AI/ML tools (e.g., JSON, CSV).
- **Workflow Orchestration:** Coordinates multiple processes, such as extracting data, transforming it, and

feeding it into an AI/ML model.

- **Error Handling:** Identifies and resolves issues during data transfers, ensuring smooth operation.

Popular Middleware Solutions

- **IBM MQ:** Facilitates secure and reliable data exchange between IBM mainframes and AI/ML tools.
- **Apache Kafka:** Handles real-time data streaming, making it ideal for AI/ML applications requiring continuous updates.
- **MuleSoft:** Provides a comprehensive integration platform with built-in connectors for mainframes and modern AI/ML systems.

Example in Practice

A financial institution uses Apache Kafka as middleware to stream transaction data from its mainframe to a fraud detection AI model. The middleware ensures data consistency and handles format conversion, enabling seamless integration.

---

3. Real-World Examples of APIs and Middleware in Action

Case Study: Enhancing Healthcare Analytics

A healthcare provider wanted to use AI/ML to predict patient admission rates based on historical data stored on mainframes. By implementing middleware to transform legacy data formats and REST APIs to connect the mainframe to an AI/ML platform, the organization achieved:

- Real-time insights into patient trends.
- Optimized resource allocation for hospital beds and staff.

Case Study: Fraud Detection in Banking

A global bank integrated an AI-powered fraud detection model with its IBM mainframe. Using IBM MQ as middleware, the bank enabled secure and reliable communication between systems, reducing fraud detection times from hours to minutes.

Why APIs and Middleware Matter

By facilitating communication between mainframes and AI/ML tools, APIs and middleware unlock the potential for:

- **Efficient Workflows:** Streamlined processes that minimize delays and reduce manual intervention.
- **Scalable Integration:** Systems capable of handling increased data volumes and computational demands.
- **Innovation Enablement:** The ability to leverage advanced AI/ML technologies without overhauling existing mainframe systems.

Conclusion

APIs and middleware are indispensable components of mainframe-AI/ML integration. APIs provide standardized interfaces for data exchange, while middleware simplifies the complexities of system interoperability. Together, they enable organizations to harness the power of AI/ML while preserving the reliability and efficiency of their mainframes.

Next, we'll explore **Best Practices for Choosing and Implementing Middleware**, offering practical strategies to maximize the effectiveness of these integration tools.

Best Practices for Choosing and Implementing Middleware

Middleware plays a critical role in connecting legacy mainframe systems with modern AI/ML tools, acting as the intermediary that enables seamless data exchange and operational interoperability. Choosing and deploying middleware effectively can significantly influence the success of your AI/ML integration efforts. This section explores the key considerations, implementation strategies, and maintenance tips for middleware, ensuring that your integration process is efficient, scalable, and future-proof.

1. Key Criteria for Evaluating Middleware Solutions

When selecting middleware, organizations should assess potential solutions based on specific technical and organizational requirements. Key evaluation criteria include:

Scalability

- Middleware should handle both current and future data volumes, ensuring that performance remains consistent as workloads increase.
- Look for solutions that support distributed processing or cloud integration to manage spikes in demand.

Compatibility

- Verify the middleware's ability to work with mainframe-specific data formats (e.g., EBCDIC, VSAM) and protocols.

- Ensure compatibility with AI/ML platforms, databases, and data pipelines, minimizing the need for additional integration layers.

Ease of Use

- Opt for middleware with user-friendly interfaces and documentation, reducing the learning curve for your IT team.
- Consider solutions that offer pre-built connectors for popular AI/ML tools and mainframe systems.

Security Features

- Evaluate middleware that provides robust encryption, access control, and data integrity features to protect sensitive information during data transfer.

Vendor Support

- Assess the quality and availability of vendor support, including training, updates, and troubleshooting services.

---

2. Implementation Strategies for Middleware

Deploying middleware effectively requires careful planning and execution to ensure minimal disruption to existing systems. Follow these strategies to streamline implementation:

Assess Current Infrastructure

- Conduct a thorough audit of your mainframe and AI/ML environments to identify integration points, potential bottlenecks, and resource requirements.

Pilot Testing

- Start with a small-scale deployment to validate the middleware's functionality and compatibility before scaling to the full system.
- Use test scenarios to evaluate performance, data integrity, and error handling capabilities.

Gradual Rollout

- Implement middleware in phases, focusing on high-priority integration points first. This approach reduces risks and provides opportunities for iterative improvement.

Customization

- Configure middleware to align with your organization's workflows, data structures, and security protocols. Customization ensures that the middleware fits seamlessly into your existing ecosystem.

Cross-Functional Collaboration

- Involve stakeholders from IT, data science, and operations teams to ensure that the middleware supports diverse requirements and objectives.

---

3. Tips for Ongoing Maintenance and Updates

Middleware requires continuous monitoring and updates to remain effective and secure. Implement the following practices to maintain optimal performance:

Regular Performance Monitoring

- Use monitoring tools to track key performance metrics, such as data transfer rates, latency, and error rates.
- Set up alerts for anomalies to address issues proactively.

Scheduled Updates

- Keep middleware up to date with the latest patches and features to maintain compatibility with evolving mainframe and AI/ML systems.

Backup and Recovery

- Implement backup solutions to protect middleware configurations and data. Ensure that recovery procedures are in place to minimize downtime during failures.

Documentation

- Maintain detailed documentation of middleware configurations, workflows, and integration points to simplify troubleshooting and onboarding.

Adapt to Changes

- Monitor advancements in middleware technologies and evolving business needs. Be prepared to upgrade or replace middleware solutions to stay competitive.

Real-World Example: Middleware Implementation in Retail

A global retail chain integrated middleware to connect its IBM mainframe with a cloud-based AI platform for inventory optimization. By following these best practices:

- **Scalability:** The middleware handled seasonal demand spikes during holiday sales.
- **Compatibility:** Pre-built connectors enabled seamless data exchange between legacy systems and modern tools.
- **Implementation:** A phased rollout ensured minimal disruption to daily operations.
- **Maintenance:** Regular updates kept the system secure and aligned with business growth.

Conclusion

Choosing and implementing middleware is a critical step in bridging the gap between mainframes and AI/ML tools. By evaluating scalability, compatibility, and ease of use, deploying middleware strategically, and maintaining it effectively, organizations can ensure smooth integration processes. These best practices empower enterprises to unlock the full potential of AI/ML without compromising the reliability and stability of their mainframe systems.

In the next section, we'll explore **Hybrid Cloud Options for AI/ML**, delving into how hybrid architectures can support scalable, secure, and efficient integration of AI/ML with mainframes.

17. Hybrid Cloud Options for AI/ML

Hybrid cloud architectures are transforming how enterprises integrate AI/ML capabilities with their mainframe environments. By combining on-premises mainframe systems with cloud-based platforms, hybrid solutions offer the best of both worlds—leveraging the reliability and performance of mainframes while tapping into the scalability and flexibility of the cloud.

This chapter explores the potential of hybrid cloud options for AI/ML, focusing on their benefits and the platforms that make integration seamless. These insights will help you understand how to use hybrid architectures to enhance your organization's ability to manage data, train models, and deploy solutions effectively.

Overview of Subtopics

1. Benefits of Hybrid Architectures for Scalability and Performance

Hybrid architectures provide a dynamic framework for scaling AI/ML workloads and improving overall system performance. In this section, we'll discuss:

- How hybrid models enable the offloading of resource-intensive tasks, such as model training, to the cloud.
- The role of hybrid environments in ensuring high availability, reliability, and cost optimization.
- Real-world scenarios where hybrid solutions have enhanced enterprise AI/ML capabilities.

Understanding these benefits will demonstrate why hybrid cloud architectures are becoming the preferred choice for enterprises balancing legacy systems with cutting-edge technologies.

2. Examples of Cloud Platforms Supporting AI/ML for Mainframes

Cloud platforms are pivotal in hybrid architectures, offering tools and services tailored for AI/ML workflows. This section will cover:

- Major platforms like **AWS**, **Microsoft Azure**, **Google Cloud Platform**, and their AI/ML services.
- Specialized offerings for mainframe integration, such as **IBM Cloud for Z** and **Oracle Cloud Infrastructure**.
- Key features, use cases, and compatibility considerations for each platform.

By examining these platforms, you'll gain practical insights into choosing the right cloud services to complement your mainframe environment and achieve your AI/ML objectives.

Why This Chapter Matters

Hybrid cloud architectures provide an essential bridge between the robustness of mainframes and the innovation-driven capabilities of cloud-based AI/ML tools. Exploring these options allows you to:

- **Enhance Scalability:** Address fluctuating workloads without overburdening your mainframe.
- **Improve Performance:** Leverage cloud computing power for faster model training and analytics.
- **Drive Innovation:** Access cutting-edge AI/ML tools while maintaining the reliability of legacy systems.

Looking Ahead

In the next sections, we'll dive deeper into the **Benefits of Hybrid Architectures for Scalability and Performance** and examine real-world **Examples of Cloud Platforms Supporting AI/ML for Mainframes**. These discussions will provide actionable insights to help you design and implement a hybrid strategy that aligns with your organization's goals.

Benefits of Hybrid Architectures for Scalability and Performance

Hybrid cloud architectures offer a robust framework for enterprises aiming to integrate AI/ML capabilities with their mainframe systems. By combining the stability and reliability of on-premises mainframes with the flexibility and scalability of the cloud, hybrid models empower organizations to optimize performance, manage costs, and drive innovation. Let's delve into the key benefits that make hybrid architectures an ideal solution for modern enterprise AI/ML workflows.

1. Offloading Resource-Intensive Tasks to the Cloud

Mainframes are designed for mission-critical, transaction-heavy workloads, but tasks such as training AI/ML models often require significant computational resources. Hybrid architectures enable organizations to:

- **Leverage Cloud Resources:** Use cloud platforms for tasks like model training and large-scale data analysis, reducing the strain on mainframe systems.
- **Dynamic Resource Allocation:** Scale cloud resources up or down based on demand, ensuring efficient use of infrastructure without over-provisioning.
- **Speed Up Workflows:** Accelerate AI/ML processes by utilizing powerful GPUs and distributed computing available in cloud environments.

Example

A financial institution uses a hybrid model to train fraud detection algorithms in the cloud, processing millions of historical transactions. Once the model is trained, it is deployed back to the mainframe for real-time fraud prevention.

---

2. Ensuring High Availability, Reliability, and Cost Optimization

Hybrid architectures strike a balance between the reliability of mainframes and the scalability of cloud environments, enabling enterprises to achieve:

- **High Availability:** By distributing workloads across on-premises and cloud systems, hybrid models reduce the risk of downtime and ensure continuous operation.
- **Reliability:** Mainframes maintain their role as the backbone of critical operations, while cloud services handle non-critical, high-complexity tasks.
- **Cost Efficiency:** Organizations can optimize costs by keeping regular operations on the mainframe and moving resource-intensive, sporadic workloads to the cloud.

Example

A healthcare provider uses a hybrid architecture to process patient data. Routine transactional operations remain on the mainframe, while AI models in the cloud analyze trends for predictive healthcare planning.

---

3. Enhancing Enterprise AI/ML Capabilities with Hybrid Solutions

Hybrid models expand the potential of AI/ML by combining the strengths of both environments:

- **Seamless Data Access:** Mainframes store vast amounts of structured data critical for AI/ML, while the cloud provides advanced tools and frameworks for analysis.
- **Innovation at Scale:** Hybrid architectures make it possible to experiment with cutting-edge AI technologies in the cloud without disrupting core mainframe operations.
- **Faster Time to Market:** By leveraging cloud-native AI/ML tools, organizations can prototype, test, and deploy solutions more quickly than relying solely on on-premises systems.

Example

A retail chain uses a hybrid cloud to analyze customer purchasing behaviors. AI/ML models are developed and trained in the cloud, then deployed to mainframes to provide personalized recommendations at point-of-sale systems.

Conclusion

Hybrid cloud architectures are becoming the preferred choice for enterprises that need to balance legacy mainframe systems with modern AI/ML technologies. By offloading resource-intensive tasks to the cloud, ensuring high availability and reliability, and enhancing AI/ML capabilities, hybrid models deliver unmatched scalability and performance.

Next, we'll explore **Examples of Cloud Platforms Supporting AI/ML for Mainframes**, examining specific tools and services that make hybrid integration seamless and efficient.

Examples of Cloud Platforms Supporting AI/ML for Mainframes

Hybrid architectures rely heavily on cloud platforms to extend the capabilities of mainframe systems. These platforms provide powerful AI/ML services, tailored solutions for mainframe integration, and the flexibility to handle diverse workloads. Let's explore the leading cloud platforms and specialized offerings that support AI/ML integration with mainframes.

1. Major Cloud Platforms and Their AI/ML Services

Amazon Web Services (AWS)

AWS offers a comprehensive suite of AI/ML tools and services designed for scalability and versatility:

- **Key Services:**
    - **Amazon SageMaker:** Enables the development, training, and deployment of ML models at scale.
    - **AWS Glue:** A serverless ETL service that simplifies data preparation.
    - **Amazon Forecast:** A service for time-series forecasting using AI/ML.
- **Use Cases:**
    - Predictive maintenance by analyzing historical performance data.
    - Fraud detection using real-time transaction monitoring.
- **Compatibility with Mainframes:**
    - AWS offers connectors and APIs for integrating

mainframe data with cloud services.
    - Tools like AWS Mainframe Modernization Service help bridge legacy systems and cloud-native applications.

Microsoft Azure

Microsoft Azure provides robust tools for enterprise AI/ML, with an emphasis on integrating with existing IT environments:

- **Key Services:**
    - **Azure Machine Learning:** A comprehensive platform for developing and managing ML models.
    - **Azure Synapse Analytics:** Facilitates data integration and analytics across large datasets.
    - **Azure Logic Apps:** Simplifies the connection of mainframes with AI/ML workflows.
- **Use Cases:**
    - Customer segmentation and recommendation engines for retail.
    - Resource optimization in manufacturing operations.
- **Compatibility with Mainframes:**
    - Seamless integration with on-premises systems via hybrid tools like Azure Arc and API Management.

Google Cloud Platform (GCP)

GCP is renowned for its cutting-edge AI/ML technologies and data processing capabilities:

- **Key Services:**
    - **Vertex AI:** A unified platform for ML operations (MLOps).
    - **BigQuery ML:** Allows ML modeling directly within a data warehouse.
    - **Cloud Data Fusion:** Provides data integration and transformation services.
- **Use Cases:**
    - Real-time analytics for supply chain optimization.
    - Personalization engines for digital marketing campaigns.
- **Compatibility with Mainframes:**
    - GCP supports integration through custom APIs and middleware solutions, enabling access to mainframe data for cloud-based processing.

---

2. Specialized Offerings for Mainframe Integration

IBM Cloud for Z

IBM's cloud platform is purpose-built for enterprises running IBM Z mainframes, ensuring seamless compatibility and advanced functionality:

- **Key Features:**
    - Direct support for COBOL and other mainframe-specific languages.
    - Pre-built connectors for mainframe data and cloud services.
    - Integration with IBM Watson AI tools for real-time analytics.
- **Use Cases:**

- Fraud detection for financial institutions.
- Operational analytics for logistics and supply chain management.

Oracle Cloud Infrastructure (OCI)

Oracle's cloud platform offers high-performance computing and specialized tools for enterprise AI/ML:

- **Key Features:**
  - AI-powered data preparation and automation through Oracle Data Science.
  - Native support for Oracle databases commonly used in mainframe environments.
  - Real-time streaming capabilities for large-scale data processing.
- **Use Cases:**
  - Predictive analytics for healthcare organizations.
  - Risk assessment models in financial services.

---

3. Key Features, Use Cases, and Compatibility Considerations

Key Features Across Platforms

- **Scalability:** All platforms offer scalable resources to handle fluctuating workloads, making them ideal for AI/ML tasks like model training and data analysis.
- **Advanced AI/ML Services:** Cutting-edge tools, including pre-trained models, deep learning frameworks, and MLOps capabilities, ensure efficiency.
- **Integration Tools:** Connectors, APIs, and middleware enable seamless data transfer between mainframes and

cloud systems.

Use Cases in Enterprise Environments

- **Financial Services:** AWS and IBM Cloud support fraud detection and compliance reporting.
- **Retail:** GCP and Azure enable personalized marketing and inventory optimization.
- **Healthcare:** Oracle Cloud facilitates predictive patient care and resource allocation.

Compatibility Considerations

- **Data Formats:** Ensure the platform supports mainframe-specific data formats like EBCDIC or VSAM, or provide transformation tools.
- **APIs:** Look for pre-built APIs to minimize custom development efforts.
- **Security and Compliance:** Choose platforms with robust security measures and compliance certifications relevant to your industry.

Conclusion

Cloud platforms are essential enablers of hybrid architectures, offering a wide range of tools to support AI/ML workflows while maintaining compatibility with mainframe systems. By understanding the unique features and capabilities of platforms like AWS, Microsoft Azure, Google Cloud, IBM Cloud for Z, and Oracle Cloud Infrastructure, organizations can select the solution that best aligns with their technical needs and business goals.

Part VI: Building and Deploying AI/ML Models

The journey from concept to deployment is where the true value of AI/ML initiatives is realized. Building and deploying AI/ML models involves a combination of technical expertise, strategic planning, and iterative refinement. For enterprises integrating these technologies into mainframe environments, this process is critical to unlocking insights, driving automation, and achieving transformative business outcomes.

Part VI focuses on the essential stages of model development, training, validation, and testing, providing actionable guidance to ensure your AI/ML initiatives are successful from the ground up.

Why This Part Matters

Building and deploying AI/ML models isn't just about technical execution; it's about aligning your efforts with business objectives, managing resources effectively, and ensuring robust, reliable results. This part of the book will:

- Demystify the processes of creating and refining AI/ML models.
- Highlight best practices for ensuring accuracy, reliability, and scalability.
- Address common challenges and offer solutions for overcoming them.

Whether you're developing your first model or refining an existing workflow, these chapters will provide a comprehensive roadmap to success.

What You'll Learn

- **The Foundations of Model Development:** Step-by-step guidance for building your first AI/ML model, including selecting tools, defining objectives, and understanding key concepts.
- **Training and Validation:** Techniques for ensuring your model learns effectively from data and delivers reliable results in real-world scenarios.
- **Controlled Testing:** Strategies for testing models in safe, controlled environments to minimize risks and optimize performance before full deployment.

How This Part Fits Into the Bigger Picture

Building and deploying AI/ML models is the culmination of the groundwork laid in earlier parts of the book. Once models are created, trained, and tested, they become the engines that drive AI-powered insights and automation in your enterprise. By approaching this process with care and rigor, you'll set the stage for successful integration with your mainframe systems and broader enterprise operations.

In the next chapter, **Developing Your First AI/ML Model**, we'll dive into the foundational steps of creating a model from scratch, providing a detailed blueprint to get you started.

18. Developing Your First AI/ML Model

Developing your first AI/ML model is a milestone in leveraging the power of artificial intelligence to solve real-world problems. While the process may seem complex, breaking it down into manageable steps and understanding the tools available can simplify the journey. This chapter provides a practical roadmap for building a basic AI/ML model, offering actionable insights and best practices to guide you through the development process.

What You'll Learn

In this chapter, we'll cover:

- A **step-by-step guide** to designing, training, and evaluating a foundational AI/ML model. This process will include defining the problem, preparing the data, choosing algorithms, and validating results.
- An overview of popular **tools and libraries** that streamline model development, with a focus on their compatibility with mainframe environments and enterprise workflows.

These topics will equip you with the foundational knowledge and confidence to start creating AI/ML solutions tailored to your organization's needs.

Overview of Subtopics

1. Step-by-Step Guide to Building a Basic Model

We'll walk through the essential stages of model development, from identifying a problem to deploying a functional model. Key steps include:

- Defining the problem and goals for the model.
- Preparing and preprocessing data to ensure quality and relevance.
- Selecting an algorithm suited to your use case.
- Training and validating the model for optimal performance.
  This structured approach will demystify the process and provide a clear pathway for beginners and experienced professionals alike.

---

2. Tools and Libraries for Model Development

Selecting the right tools can simplify development and enhance productivity. We'll explore:

- Open-source frameworks like TensorFlow, PyTorch, and Scikit-learn, known for their flexibility and robust features.
- Enterprise-grade solutions like SAS Viya and IBM Watson, designed for scalability and integration with mainframe systems.
- Supporting tools for data visualization, preprocessing, and deployment.
  Understanding these tools and their capabilities will help you choose the best fit for your projects.

Why This Chapter Matters

Building your first AI/ML model is not just a technical exercise—it's an opportunity to see the tangible impact of AI in action. By following a structured process and leveraging the right tools, you can create solutions that address real business challenges, unlock insights, and drive efficiency.

In the next section, we'll dive into the **Step-by-Step Guide to Building a Basic Model**, where we'll break down the model development process into clear, actionable stages to get you started.

Step-by-Step Guide to Building a Basic Model

Developing a machine learning (ML) model may initially seem daunting, but by breaking it down into clear, actionable stages, the process becomes manageable and logical. Each step builds upon the previous one, ensuring your model is tailored to solve a specific problem effectively. Here's how to approach it:

1. Defining the Problem and Goals for the Model

The first step in building a successful ML model is understanding what you're trying to achieve. This involves:

- **Identifying the Problem:** Determine the specific issue you want to solve. For example, are you predicting equipment failures, detecting anomalies, or optimizing resource allocation?
- **Setting Clear Goals:** Define measurable objectives. For instance, "Improve fraud detection accuracy by 10%" or "Reduce downtime by predicting system failures."
- **Understanding Business Impact:** Connect the model's purpose to organizational goals, such as cost savings, operational efficiency, or enhanced customer experience.

Example

A financial institution might want to predict customer churn. The goal is to identify at-risk customers and offer them targeted retention campaigns, reducing churn by a defined percentage.

2. Preparing and Preprocessing Data

High-quality data is the foundation of any ML model. The data preparation stage ensures your model has accurate, relevant, and structured information to learn from. Steps include:

- **Collecting Data:** Gather data from all relevant sources, such as mainframe logs, transactional databases, or customer profiles.
- **Cleaning Data:** Remove duplicates, fill missing values, and correct inconsistencies to avoid errors during training.
- **Feature Engineering:** Create new variables (features) that enhance the model's predictive power, such as combining transactional data with customer demographics.
- **Normalization and Scaling:** Ensure data is in a consistent format and range, particularly if using algorithms sensitive to numerical scales.

Example

In a predictive maintenance use case, data from sensors, historical maintenance logs, and system performance metrics might need to be consolidated and cleaned before training the model.

---

3. Selecting an Algorithm Suited to Your Use Case

Choosing the right algorithm is critical for achieving optimal results. Factors to consider include:

- **Nature of the Problem:** Is it a classification task (e.g., fraud detection), regression (e.g., predicting sales), or clustering (e.g., customer segmentation)?
- **Data Size and Complexity:** Some algorithms, like

decision trees, handle smaller datasets well, while others, like deep learning models, thrive on large-scale data.

- **Model Interpretability:** For regulated industries, algorithms like linear regression or decision trees are easier to explain, while neural networks might be more powerful but less interpretable.

Common Algorithms

- **Classification:** Logistic regression, decision trees, random forests.
- **Regression:** Linear regression, support vector machines.
- **Clustering:** K-means, hierarchical clustering.
- **Deep Learning:** Neural networks for complex, high-dimensional problems.

Example

For a churn prediction model, a random forest classifier might be chosen for its balance of accuracy and interpretability.

---

4. Training and Validating the Model

This stage involves teaching the model to recognize patterns in the data and ensuring it performs well on unseen data. Steps include:

- **Splitting Data:** Divide the dataset into training and testing sets, typically 70-30 or 80-20.
- **Model Training:** Use the training set to teach the model by minimizing errors through iterative learning processes.
- **Validation:** Evaluate the model's performance on the testing set to measure accuracy, precision, recall, or other relevant metrics.

- **Tuning Hyperparameters:** Adjust settings like learning rate, number of trees, or regularization parameters to optimize performance.

Example

For fraud detection, the model might be trained on historical transaction data, then validated against recent transactions to ensure it accurately identifies fraudulent patterns.

---

5. Deployment

Once trained and validated, the model is ready to be integrated into a production environment:

- **Integrate with Mainframes:** Use APIs or middleware to deploy the model, allowing it to analyze live data from mainframe systems.
- **Monitor and Iterate:** Continuously track the model's performance and update it with new data to maintain accuracy over time.

Example

A deployed churn prediction model could be integrated into a CRM system, triggering automated retention campaigns for at-risk customers in real-time.

Conclusion

This structured approach simplifies the process of building an ML model, ensuring each stage is deliberate and purposeful. From defining the problem to deployment, every step is designed to maximize the model's relevance, accuracy, and impact.

In the next section, we'll explore **Tools and Libraries for Model Development**, detailing the platforms and frameworks that can streamline this process and align with mainframe environments.

Tools and Libraries for Model Development

The tools and libraries you choose for AI/ML model development significantly impact the efficiency, scalability, and success of your projects. Whether you're building simple models or implementing complex AI systems, selecting the right tools is critical to streamline workflows and align with your enterprise needs. This section explores some of the most popular tools and their capabilities, focusing on open-source frameworks, enterprise-grade solutions, and supporting utilities.

1. Open-Source Frameworks

Open-source frameworks are widely used in AI/ML development due to their flexibility, community support, and robust feature sets. Let's look at some of the most popular options:

TensorFlow

- **Overview:** TensorFlow is a powerful library for numerical computation and large-scale machine learning. It supports deep learning and neural network models with an easy-to-use interface.
- **Key Features:**
  - Supports complex workflows like training, testing, and deploying models.
  - Provides pre-built tools for image recognition, natural language processing (NLP), and time-series analysis.
  - Offers TensorFlow Serving for deploying models

in production environments.

- **Use Cases:** Deep learning applications, such as image classification and speech recognition.

PyTorch

- **Overview:** PyTorch is known for its dynamic computation graph and intuitive debugging, making it a favorite among researchers and developers.
- **Key Features:**
    - Simplifies the creation of neural networks with its user-friendly API.
    - Integrates seamlessly with Python's ecosystem for data manipulation and visualization.
    - Supports distributed training for large datasets.
- **Use Cases:** Research-heavy projects, NLP, and computer vision tasks.

Scikit-learn

- **Overview:** Scikit-learn is a versatile library for traditional machine learning algorithms.
- **Key Features:**
    - Provides easy-to-use implementations of regression, classification, and clustering algorithms.
    - Includes tools for preprocessing, cross-validation, and model evaluation.
    - Suitable for smaller datasets and quick prototyping.
- **Use Cases:** Predictive analytics, anomaly detection, and

customer segmentation.

---

2. Enterprise-Grade Solutions

For organizations requiring scalability, integration with existing systems, and enterprise-level support, commercial solutions provide advanced features tailored to business needs.

SAS Viya

- **Overview:** SAS Viya is a cloud-based analytics platform designed for AI/ML and data science.
- **Key Features:**
    - Built-in support for data preparation, model training, and deployment.
    - Integrates seamlessly with mainframe systems for real-time data analysis.
    - Provides advanced visualization tools for interpreting model results.
- **Use Cases:** Risk analysis, fraud detection, and customer behavior modeling in enterprise environments.

IBM Watson

- **Overview:** IBM Watson offers a suite of AI tools with a focus on enterprise applications.
- **Key Features:**
    - Pre-trained models for NLP, computer vision, and automated workflows.
    - Tight integration with IBM Z mainframes through APIs and middleware.
    - Tools for explainable AI to meet regulatory

compliance requirements.

- **Use Cases:** Customer service chatbots, predictive maintenance, and operational analytics.

---

3. Supporting Tools

Beyond core frameworks, supporting tools enhance the efficiency of data preparation, visualization, and deployment processes.

Data Visualization

- **Tableau:** Interactive dashboards for exploring and presenting insights.
- **Matplotlib/Seaborn:** Python libraries for creating static and dynamic visualizations.

Data Preprocessing

- **Pandas:** A Python library for data manipulation and cleaning.
- **Apache Nifi:** A tool for automating data integration workflows across systems.

Deployment Tools

- **MLflow:** Manages the lifecycle of machine learning models, from experimentation to deployment.
- **Kubeflow:** Provides an end-to-end pipeline for deploying ML models on Kubernetes clusters.

Choosing the Right Tools for Your Projects

Factors to Consider:

- **Complexity of the Use Case:** Use TensorFlow or PyTorch for deep learning, and Scikit-learn for simpler models.
- **Integration Needs:** Enterprise-grade solutions like SAS Viya or IBM Watson are ideal for seamless mainframe integration.
- **Budget and Resources:** Open-source frameworks offer cost-effective solutions, but enterprise tools provide additional support and scalability.

Compatibility with Mainframes:

Ensure that your chosen tools can handle mainframe-specific data formats, integrate with APIs, and support hybrid cloud environments for scalable workflows.

Conclusion

By understanding the capabilities and use cases of these tools and libraries, you can make informed decisions that align with your organization's goals and technical infrastructure. In the next section, we'll explore the practical steps of **Training and Validating Models**, focusing on techniques to improve model accuracy and reliability.

19. Training and Validating Models

Training and validating models are critical stages in the machine learning (ML) lifecycle, transforming raw data into actionable insights. These processes ensure that your model not only learns from the data but also performs reliably in real-world scenarios. For enterprises leveraging mainframe systems, effective training and validation are essential to achieve accuracy, efficiency, and scalability.

What You'll Learn

This chapter explores:

- **Techniques for Training Models with Mainframe Data:** Adapting traditional training methods to accommodate the unique characteristics of mainframe datasets, such as legacy formats and transactional nature.
- **Methods for Validating Accuracy and Performance:** Ensuring that models deliver consistent and accurate results by employing rigorous evaluation techniques tailored to enterprise environments.

These subtopics will provide actionable strategies for optimizing the training process and ensuring that models are both effective and reliable.

Overview of Subtopics

1. Techniques for Training Models with Mainframe Data

Training ML models on mainframe data requires addressing challenges like data preprocessing, scale, and system integration. We'll explore:

- How to preprocess and structure mainframe data for ML workflows.
- Training methodologies, including batch training and incremental updates, that work well with mainframe datasets.
- Practical tips for leveraging hybrid cloud environments to enhance computational efficiency during training.

---

2. Methods for Validating Accuracy and Performance

Validation ensures that the trained model performs well on unseen data and meets business objectives. We'll discuss:

- Evaluation metrics such as precision, recall, F1 score, and mean squared error, tailored to different use cases.
- Cross-validation techniques to ensure robust performance across diverse datasets.
- Strategies to identify and address issues like overfitting or underfitting, which can compromise model reliability.

Why This Chapter Matters

Without effective training, your model risks being underpowered or overfit, limiting its practical utility. Similarly, without rigorous validation, you cannot guarantee that the model will perform reliably in production. By mastering these stages, you'll build models that deliver consistent, high-quality results, whether predicting system failures, detecting anomalies, or optimizing workloads.

In the next section, **Techniques for Training Models with Mainframe Data**, we'll dive into the specifics of preparing and leveraging mainframe datasets to create high-performing AI/ML models.

Techniques for Training Models with Mainframe Data

Training machine learning (ML) models using mainframe data involves navigating unique challenges such as legacy formats, high transaction volumes, and stringent operational requirements. By adopting specialized techniques, organizations can ensure effective model training while optimizing for performance and scalability. Here's how to approach the task:

1. Preprocessing and Structuring Mainframe Data for ML Workflows

Mainframe data often resides in legacy formats or complex transactional systems, requiring meticulous preprocessing to prepare it for machine learning workflows.

Key Steps in Data Preprocessing:

- **Format Conversion:** Translate legacy formats such as EBCDIC or VSAM into modern formats like CSV or Parquet, which are compatible with ML tools.
- **Data Cleaning:** Handle missing values, correct inconsistencies, and remove duplicates to ensure data integrity.
- **Feature Engineering:** Create meaningful features by deriving insights from raw data. For instance, combine multiple transactional attributes into a composite feature, such as "average transaction value per customer."
- **Normalization and Scaling:** Adjust data to a uniform

scale to prevent biases, especially when using algorithms sensitive to magnitude differences.

Practical Example:

In a workload optimization project, raw transactional logs from the mainframe can be transformed into structured datasets highlighting key metrics like CPU usage, memory allocation, and queue wait times. These metrics can serve as features for the ML model.

2. Training Methodologies for Mainframe Datasets

Different training approaches suit various use cases, especially when handling large-scale mainframe data.

Batch Training:

- **What It Is:** The model is trained using a large, static dataset in one go.
- **Advantages:** Suitable for use cases with stable datasets and where periodic retraining is sufficient.
- **Challenges:** Resource-intensive; requires careful preparation of the dataset to avoid overfitting.
- **Example Use Case:** Predictive maintenance based on historical equipment failure data.

Incremental Training:

- **What It Is:** The model is updated incrementally as new data becomes available, without re-training from scratch.
- **Advantages:** Ideal for dynamic environments where data evolves over time.
- **Challenges:** Requires robust algorithms capable of handling incremental updates, such as online learning

techniques.
- **Example Use Case:** Fraud detection, where models need to adapt to emerging fraud patterns continuously.

Mini-Batch Training:

- **What It Is:** The dataset is divided into smaller batches, and the model is trained iteratively on these chunks.
- **Advantages:** Combines the scalability of batch training with the adaptability of incremental methods.
- **Example Use Case:** Resource allocation models, where computational efficiency is critical.

---

3. Leveraging Hybrid Cloud Environments for Computational Efficiency

Mainframes are not always optimized for computationally intensive tasks like model training. Hybrid cloud environments provide scalable infrastructure for these workloads.

Key Benefits of Hybrid Cloud Training:

- **Scalability:** Use cloud resources for intensive operations like deep learning while keeping sensitive data within the mainframe environment.
- **Cost Efficiency:** Offload only the computationally heavy tasks, minimizing infrastructure expenses.
- **Enhanced Speed:** Parallelize training processes across cloud nodes to reduce training time.

Workflow for Hybrid Cloud Training:

1. **Data Extraction:** Export relevant data from the mainframe to a secure cloud environment.
2. **Preprocessing in the Cloud:** Leverage cloud-based tools like Apache Spark or AWS Glue for preprocessing at scale.
3. **Model Training:** Use platforms like TensorFlow on Google Cloud AI Platform or SageMaker on AWS for efficient training.
4. **Model Deployment:** Integrate the trained model back into the mainframe system via APIs or middleware.

Practical Example:

A bank might export its transactional data to a cloud environment to train a model for fraud detection using a deep learning framework. Once trained, the model can be deployed back to the mainframe for real-time fraud analysis.

Conclusion

Training ML models on mainframe data requires careful attention to data preparation, choice of training methodology, and infrastructure optimization. By preprocessing data effectively, selecting the right training approach, and leveraging hybrid cloud environments, organizations can unlock the full potential of their mainframe data in AI/ML workflows.

In the next section, **Methods for Validating Accuracy and Performance**, we'll explore how to ensure that trained models perform reliably and meet organizational objectives.

Methods for Validating Accuracy and Performance

Validation is a critical step in the machine learning (ML) lifecycle, ensuring that the model is reliable, accurate, and aligned with business objectives. Effective validation techniques minimize errors, optimize performance, and provide insights into areas for improvement. Let's explore how to validate ML models, focusing on evaluation metrics, cross-validation techniques, and strategies to address common issues.

1. Evaluation Metrics Tailored to Use Cases

Different ML problems require different evaluation metrics to assess model performance effectively. Choosing the right metric ensures that the model meets the specific needs of the application.

Classification Metrics:

- **Precision:** Measures the proportion of correctly predicted positive cases among all predicted positive cases. Critical for tasks like fraud detection, where false positives can lead to unnecessary investigations. Precision=True PositivesTrue Positives + False Positives\text{Precision} = \frac{\text{True Positives}}{\text{True Positives + False Positives}}Precision=True Positives + False PositivesTrue Positives
- **Recall:** Measures the proportion of correctly predicted positive cases among all actual positive cases. Important for anomaly detection to ensure all critical cases are identified.

Recall=True PositivesTrue Positives + False Negatives\text{Recall} = \frac{\text{True Positives}}{\text{True Positives + False Negatives}}Recall=True Positives + False NegativesTrue Positives

- **F1 Score:** The harmonic mean of precision and recall, balancing both metrics. Useful when both false positives and false negatives carry significant costs. F1 Score=2·Precision·RecallPrecision + Recall\text{F1 Score} = 2 \cdot \frac{\text{Precision} \cdot \text{Recall}}{\text{Precision + Recall}}F1 Score=2·Precision + RecallPrecision·Recall

Regression Metrics:

- **Mean Squared Error (MSE):** Measures the average squared difference between predicted and actual values, emphasizing larger errors. Ideal for predicting numeric outcomes, such as system load. MSE=1n∑i=1n(yi−y^i)2\text{MSE} = \frac{1}{n} \sum_{i=1}^n (y_i - \hat{y}_i)^2MSE=n1i=1∑n(yi−y^i)2
- **R-Squared:** Indicates how well the model explains the variance in the data, providing a measure of goodness-of-fit. R2=1−Sum of Squares of ResidualsTotal Sum of SquaresR^2 = 1 - \frac{\text{Sum of Squares of Residuals}}{\text{Total Sum of Squares}}R2=1−Total Sum of SquaresSum of Squares of Residuals

Practical Example:

For a predictive maintenance model, precision ensures that resources aren't wasted on false alarms, while recall ensures critical failures are flagged.

2. Cross-Validation Techniques

Cross-validation involves splitting the dataset into multiple subsets to test the model's performance across various data configurations. This ensures robustness and prevents overfitting to a single dataset.

Common Techniques:

- **K-Fold Cross-Validation:**
  - The dataset is divided into kkk equal-sized folds.
  - The model is trained on k−1k-1k−1 folds and validated on the remaining fold, repeated kkk times.
  - Provides a comprehensive assessment of model performance.
- **Stratified K-Fold:**
  - Ensures each fold has a similar distribution of classes, improving reliability for imbalanced datasets.
- **Leave-One-Out Cross-Validation (LOOCV):**
  - Uses one data point for validation and the rest for training.
  - Useful for small datasets but computationally intensive.

Practical Example:

In a workload optimization scenario, stratified K-fold can ensure that each fold contains an appropriate mix of high and low-load periods.

3. Addressing Overfitting and Underfitting

Models must strike a balance between being too complex (overfitting) and too simple (underfitting) to generalize effectively.

Overfitting:

- **Definition:** The model performs well on training data but poorly on unseen data because it has memorized the training set.
- **Indicators:** High training accuracy but low validation accuracy.
- **Solutions:**
    - Regularization techniques (e.g., L1/L2 penalties) to penalize overly complex models.
    - Reduce model complexity (e.g., fewer layers or parameters).
    - Increase the size of the training dataset through data augmentation.

Underfitting:

- **Definition:** The model fails to capture the underlying patterns in the data, resulting in poor performance on both training and validation sets.
- **Indicators:** Low accuracy on both training and validation datasets.
- **Solutions:**
    - Use a more complex algorithm or add features to improve model capacity.
    - Extend training time to allow the model to learn better.
    - Tune hyperparameters for better alignment with the data.

Conclusion

Validation ensures your model is not only accurate but also reliable and scalable for production use. By choosing appropriate metrics, employing robust cross-validation techniques, and addressing overfitting or underfitting, you can build models that consistently meet business objectives.

In the next section, **Testing AI/ML Models in a Controlled Environment**, we'll discuss how to safely evaluate models in a test environment before deploying them into production systems.

20. Testing AI/ML Models in a Controlled Environment

Testing is a crucial phase in the AI/ML workflow, ensuring that models perform as expected before they are deployed into production. A controlled environment allows organizations to evaluate model behavior, reliability, and scalability without risking disruptions to live systems. For enterprises leveraging mainframes, this step is particularly critical, as these systems often handle sensitive, high-value operations.

What You'll Learn

This chapter will focus on:

- **Setting Up a Safe Test Environment:** How to create a testing setup that mirrors production conditions, enabling thorough and risk-free model evaluation.
- **Evaluating Model Performance and Identifying Improvements:** Techniques for assessing model accuracy, robustness, and adaptability, as well as strategies for iterating on improvements.

These subtopics will guide you through the processes of validating your model's readiness and refining its capabilities for optimal deployment.

Overview of Subtopics

1. Setting Up a Safe Test Environment

To ensure effective testing, a robust and isolated environment is essential. We'll explore:

- The importance of creating a sandbox environment that mimics production settings without compromising operational systems.
- Strategies for simulating real-world conditions, including live data streams and concurrent workloads.
- Best practices for incorporating tools that monitor and log test outcomes, providing actionable insights for model refinement.

---

2. Evaluating Model Performance and Identifying Improvements

Testing goes beyond validating accuracy; it's about ensuring that the model meets all functional and non-functional requirements. We'll discuss:

- Key performance metrics to assess model efficacy in a mainframe context, such as latency, throughput, and error rates.
- Stress-testing techniques to evaluate how the model performs under high loads or edge cases.
- Iterative improvement methods, including error analysis and hyperparameter tuning, to address identified weaknesses.

Why This Chapter Matters

For enterprises, the stakes of deploying an untested or underperforming model are high—ranging from operational inefficiencies to reputational damage. By mastering the concepts in this chapter, you'll ensure that your AI/ML models are not only accurate but also reliable, scalable, and aligned with organizational goals.

In the next section, **Setting Up a Safe Test Environment**, we'll delve into the practical steps for creating an effective and secure testing setup that minimizes risks and maximizes insights.

Setting Up a Safe Test Environment

Testing AI/ML models in a controlled environment is critical to ensuring their reliability, scalability, and effectiveness before deployment. A safe test environment allows you to rigorously evaluate model performance without disrupting live systems. Here, we'll explore the essential steps to create such an environment, strategies to simulate real-world conditions, and the tools required to monitor and refine your models.

1. The Importance of a Sandbox Environment

A sandbox environment is an isolated testing space that replicates production settings, enabling safe experimentation with no risk to actual operations.

Why It Matters:

- **Minimized Risk:** Ensures that bugs, crashes, or inefficiencies in the model do not affect live systems or end users.
- **Replication of Production Scenarios:** Allows you to evaluate model performance in conditions that closely resemble real-world operations.
- **Cost-Efficiency:** Prevents costly disruptions to critical mainframe processes by isolating testing activities.

Key Features of a Sandbox Environment:

- **Data Fidelity:** Uses anonymized or synthetic data that mimics the characteristics of live data without exposing sensitive information.

- **Controlled Access:** Limits access to the environment to authorized personnel, maintaining security and compliance.
- **Rollback Capability:** Enables the reversal of changes or tests to maintain a clean slate for iterative testing.

---

2. Simulating Real-World Conditions

The accuracy of your test results depends on how closely your environment mirrors production scenarios. Effective simulation strategies include:

Live Data Streams:

- **What It Involves:** Feeding real-time or near-real-time data into the test environment to evaluate how the model handles dynamic inputs.
- **Applications:** Testing anomaly detection models by simulating real-time transaction data from a financial mainframe system.
- **Best Practices:**
    - Use secure pipelines to anonymize sensitive data before introducing it into the test environment.
    - Introduce noise or randomness to replicate real-world variability.

Concurrent Workloads:

- **What It Involves:** Simulating the concurrent execution of tasks, transactions, or processes to test how the model performs under realistic load conditions.

- **Applications:** Evaluating workload optimization models by introducing multiple simultaneous jobs with varying resource demands.
- **Best Practices:**
    - Use workload generators to simulate traffic patterns, user interactions, or system demands.
    - Gradually increase load to identify performance thresholds and bottlenecks.

Failure Scenarios:

- **What It Involves:** Introducing faults or anomalies, such as incomplete data streams or hardware interruptions, to assess model robustness.
- **Applications:** Testing predictive maintenance models by simulating hardware failures based on historical patterns.
- **Best Practices:**
    - Automate failure scenarios using chaos engineering tools to stress-test model resilience.
    - Document model behavior and recovery time during these tests.

---

3. Best Practices for Monitoring and Logging

Testing without thorough monitoring and logging is incomplete. Effective tools and practices provide actionable insights that guide model refinement.

Monitoring Tools:

- **Real-Time Dashboards:** Tools like Grafana or Prometheus for visualizing metrics such as latency, throughput, and error rates during testing.

- **Application Performance Monitoring (APM):** Software like Dynatrace or New Relic to monitor the overall performance of applications integrated with the model.

Logging Practices:

- **Comprehensive Logs:** Ensure logs capture data inputs, model predictions, resource utilization, and error messages.
- **Structured Formats:** Use standardized formats like JSON or XML to make logs easier to parse and analyze.
- **Retention Policies:** Retain logs long enough for post-test analysis but implement cleanup protocols to manage storage costs.

Actionable Insights:

- **Error Analysis:** Identify common failure points and their root causes.
- **Performance Metrics:** Assess whether the model meets predefined benchmarks for accuracy, speed, and resource efficiency.
- **Improvement Recommendations:** Use insights to fine-tune hyperparameters, algorithms, or data preprocessing techniques.

Conclusion

A safe and robust test environment is the foundation for ensuring your AI/ML models perform reliably in production. By creating an isolated sandbox, simulating realistic conditions, and leveraging monitoring and logging tools, you can identify potential issues early and refine your models effectively.

In the next section, **Evaluating Model Performance and Identifying Improvements**, we'll explore the metrics, techniques, and strategies for assessing how well your model performs and iteratively enhancing its capabilities.

Evaluating Model Performance and Identifying Improvements

Evaluating model performance is a multi-dimensional process that ensures your AI/ML system meets both functional and non-functional requirements. It's not just about achieving high accuracy but also about ensuring that the model integrates seamlessly, operates efficiently, and remains reliable under diverse conditions. This section delves into the metrics, testing techniques, and iterative improvement strategies essential for robust model evaluation and refinement.

1. Key Performance Metrics in a Mainframe Context

Mainframe systems demand not only accuracy but also adherence to specific operational benchmarks. The following metrics are critical for assessing model efficacy:

Functional Metrics:

- **Accuracy:** Measures the percentage of correct predictions relative to the total number of predictions. Ideal for tasks like fraud detection or predictive maintenance. Accuracy=Correct PredictionsTotal Predictions\text{Accuracy} = \frac{\text{Correct Predictions}}{\text{Total Predictions}}Accuracy=Total PredictionsCorrect Predictions
- **Precision and Recall:** Evaluate the model's ability to avoid false positives (precision) and capture true positives (recall), especially critical for anomaly detection and security use cases.

- **F1 Score:** The harmonic mean of precision and recall, balancing both aspects in scenarios where both false positives and false negatives carry consequences.

Non-Functional Metrics:

- **Latency:** Measures the time the model takes to generate a prediction. For real-time systems, low latency is essential.
- **Throughput:** The number of predictions the model can handle per second, reflecting its ability to scale during high-demand periods.
- **Error Rates:** Tracks the frequency of incorrect predictions or system errors during operation, including out-of-boundary predictions.

---

2. Stress-Testing Techniques

Stress testing evaluates a model's robustness under extreme or edge-case scenarios, ensuring it can handle unexpected challenges.

High Load Testing:

- **What It Involves:** Simulating large volumes of data or concurrent requests to assess scalability.
- **Use Case:** Testing a workload optimization model by simulating peak traffic periods or batch processing demands.
- **Outcome:** Identifies potential bottlenecks in processing pipelines, enabling optimization before deployment.

Edge-Case Scenarios:

- **What It Involves:** Introducing unusual or rare data patterns to test the model's ability to handle anomalies.
- **Use Case:** Feeding unusual transaction sequences into a fraud detection model to evaluate its adaptability.
- **Outcome:** Ensures that the model does not produce inaccurate or unpredictable results in rare scenarios.

Resilience Testing:

- **What It Involves:** Simulating system failures, incomplete data streams, or sudden workload shifts.
- **Use Case:** Testing the model's behavior during temporary data loss or unexpected spikes in demand.
- **Outcome:** Verifies the model's ability to recover and maintain performance during disruptions.

---

3. Iterative Improvement Methods

Once testing reveals weaknesses, iterative refinement is critical to improve model performance and reliability.

Error Analysis:

- **Identify Failure Patterns:** Examine incorrect predictions to uncover recurring errors or biases in the model.
- **Root Cause Analysis:** Determine whether errors stem from data quality, feature selection, or algorithmic limitations.
- **Actionable Insights:** Adjust data preprocessing steps, retrain with additional features, or fine-tune model architecture to address specific errors.

Hyperparameter Tuning:

- **Definition:** Adjusting parameters that control the learning process, such as learning rate, batch size, or regularization strength.
- **Techniques:**
    - **Grid Search:** Systematically testing all combinations of predefined parameter values.
    - **Random Search:** Exploring a random subset of parameter combinations to save time while still improving performance.
    - **Bayesian Optimization:** Using probabilistic models to find the optimal set of parameters efficiently.
- **Outcome:** Maximizes model performance while minimizing overfitting or underfitting.

Retraining with Augmented Data:

- **Expand Training Sets:** Include more diverse or synthetic data to improve model generalization.
- **Handle Data Imbalances:** Use techniques like oversampling underrepresented classes or generating synthetic data with algorithms like SMOTE.
- **Outcome:** Enhances the model's ability to generalize across a wider range of scenarios.

Conclusion

Evaluating model performance is about ensuring not only accuracy but also robustness, scalability, and reliability in real-world scenarios. By leveraging comprehensive metrics, rigorous stress testing, and iterative improvements, organizations can fine-tune their models to deliver maximum value.

Part VII: Implementation and Optimization

AI/ML integration is not a one-time event but an ongoing journey that evolves as technology, data, and organizational needs change. After building and testing your models, the focus shifts to implementing them effectively and optimizing their performance to deliver long-term value.

This part of the book will guide you through the critical steps required to scale AI/ML solutions, automate workflows, and deploy models successfully. We'll explore strategies for ensuring seamless integration into mainframe environments while maintaining operational stability and maximizing efficiency.

What You'll Learn in This Section

Scaling AI/ML Solutions

Scaling involves transitioning from proof-of-concept models to full-scale implementations that can handle enterprise-level workloads. This includes optimizing resource allocation, ensuring high availability, and adapting to increasing demands.

Automating Workflows with AI/ML

Automation is one of the most transformative benefits of AI/ML. This section will explore how to integrate AI/ML into routine processes to reduce manual effort, improve accuracy, and accelerate decision-making across mainframe operations.

Best Practices for Deployment

Deploying AI/ML solutions in production requires careful planning and execution. We'll cover strategies for minimizing downtime, managing risks, and ensuring continuous monitoring and optimization.

Why This Section Matters

The true value of AI/ML lies not just in creating models but in effectively applying them to solve real-world problems. This section provides a roadmap for taking your AI/ML solutions from the lab to live environments, ensuring they deliver measurable and sustainable benefits.

In the next chapter, **Scaling AI/ML Solutions**, we'll delve into the strategies for expanding your AI/ML capabilities to support enterprise-wide adoption.

21. Scaling AI/ML Solutions

Scaling AI/ML solutions is the bridge between proof-of-concept projects and enterprise-wide adoption. While pilot projects validate the potential of AI/ML technologies, scaling ensures these solutions can handle the demands of real-world environments, delivering value across the organization.

In this chapter, we'll explore the essential steps for scaling AI/ML solutions, focusing on how to expand their scope while maintaining operational efficiency and system reliability.

What You'll Learn

1. Transitioning from Pilot Projects to Full-Scale Implementations

Pilot projects are a controlled way to test AI/ML capabilities on a smaller scale, but transitioning to enterprise-wide use introduces new challenges. We'll discuss:

- The steps involved in moving from a localized deployment to full-scale integration.
- How to address scalability concerns, such as increased data volumes, user access, and computational demands.
- Lessons learned from pilot projects that can inform the scaling process.

2. Managing Resource Allocation and Stability

Scaling AI/ML solutions requires careful resource management to ensure stability and performance. We'll cover:

- Techniques for allocating computational and storage resources efficiently, particularly in hybrid environments.
- Strategies for maintaining system stability during scaling, including load balancing and monitoring.
- The importance of aligning resource planning with long-term organizational goals.

Why This Chapter Matters

Successfully scaling AI/ML solutions transforms them from experimental tools into core components of your business strategy. By understanding the complexities and challenges involved, you'll be better equipped to achieve scalable, stable, and impactful AI/ML implementations.

In the next section, **Transitioning from Pilot Projects to Full-Scale Implementations**, we'll explore how to expand your AI/ML efforts beyond initial experiments and into enterprise-wide adoption.

Transitioning from Pilot Projects to Full-Scale Implementations

Transitioning from a pilot project to a full-scale AI/ML implementation is a pivotal step in maximizing the impact of your investment. While pilot projects allow organizations to test the feasibility of AI/ML models on a small scale, enterprise-wide deployment introduces complexities that require careful planning and execution.

Steps to Move from Pilot to Full-Scale Integration

1. Evaluate Pilot Project Results

- **Key Metrics Review:** Assess the success of the pilot based on predefined KPIs such as accuracy, efficiency gains, and cost reductions.
- **Stakeholder Feedback:** Collect insights from teams involved in the pilot to identify challenges and opportunities.
- **Scalability Analysis:** Determine whether the approach used in the pilot can be scaled without significant redesign.

2. Build an Expansion Plan

- **Define Objectives:** Clearly outline the goals of scaling, such as broader adoption, higher throughput, or expanded functionality.
- **Resource Assessment:** Evaluate the hardware, software, and personnel resources required for full-scale deployment.

- **Implementation Phases:** Break the scaling process into manageable stages, such as regional rollouts or departmental expansions, to mitigate risks.

3. Secure Stakeholder Buy-In

- **Leadership Approval:** Present pilot results and scaling plans to secure executive support and funding.
- **Team Alignment:** Ensure that cross-functional teams, including IT, data science, and operations, are aligned with the scaling strategy.

Addressing Scalability Concerns

1. Increased Data Volumes

- **Challenge:** Scaling requires handling larger datasets, which may introduce storage, processing, and retrieval complexities.
- **Solutions:**
    - Leverage hybrid cloud environments to manage data overflow.
    - Optimize data pipelines to reduce latency and improve throughput.

2. User Access

- **Challenge:** A full-scale deployment often involves multiple users or departments accessing the system simultaneously.
- **Solutions:**
    - Implement robust user management systems with

    role-based access controls (RBAC).
  - Design systems to handle concurrent requests without compromising performance.

3. Computational Demands

- **Challenge:** Scaling may increase the need for computational power, particularly for training or real-time inference.
- **Solutions:**
  - Adopt distributed computing frameworks, such as Apache Spark or TensorFlow Distributed.
  - Use hardware accelerators like GPUs or TPUs to speed up processing.

Lessons Learned from Pilot Projects

1. Address Weaknesses Early

- Use insights from the pilot to identify bottlenecks or issues that could impede scaling.
- For example, if the pilot revealed data integration challenges, resolve these before expanding.

2. Standardize Processes

- Develop repeatable workflows for tasks like data preprocessing, model deployment, and monitoring to ensure consistency during scaling.

3. Monitor Early-Stage Scaling

- Treat initial phases of scaling as an extension of the pilot, using extensive monitoring to refine processes and address unexpected challenges.

Conclusion

Transitioning from pilot projects to full-scale AI/ML implementations is a strategic effort that requires careful planning, resource alignment, and adaptability. By following a structured approach and leveraging lessons from the pilot phase, organizations can overcome scalability challenges and unlock the full potential of their AI/ML investments.

In the next section, **Managing Resource Allocation and Stability**, we'll explore strategies to ensure efficient resource management and system reliability during scaling.

Managing Resource Allocation and Stability

Scaling AI/ML solutions introduces increased demands on computational, storage, and network resources. Effective resource management ensures that performance and stability are maintained as the system grows to accommodate larger datasets, more users, and expanded use cases. This section focuses on strategies and techniques to allocate resources efficiently, maintain system stability, and align resource planning with long-term organizational objectives.

1. Allocating Computational and Storage Resources Efficiently

Key Challenges

- **Compute-Intensive Workloads:** Training and inference for AI/ML models require significant computational power, especially for large datasets and complex models.
- **Data Storage Requirements:** Mainframe environments often manage vast amounts of transactional data, which must be securely stored and readily accessible for AI/ML processing.

Strategies for Efficient Allocation

- **Hybrid Environments:** Leverage a hybrid architecture that combines on-premises mainframe systems with cloud services. This allows resource-intensive tasks, like model training, to be offloaded to the cloud while retaining critical data on secure mainframe systems.

- **Scalable Infrastructure:** Use elastic resources in cloud platforms (e.g., AWS EC2, Azure VM, Google Compute Engine) to dynamically scale up or down based on demand.
- **Data Tiering:** Implement a tiered storage system to separate frequently accessed data from archival data. Store active data in high-performance systems and move less-used data to cost-effective storage solutions.
- **Optimized Pipelines:** Streamline data pipelines to reduce duplication and inefficiencies in data processing.

---

2. Maintaining System Stability During Scaling

Key Challenges

- **Increased Traffic:** As AI/ML systems scale, more users, applications, and processes interact with the models, creating higher traffic loads.
- **Complex Dependencies:** Integrating AI/ML into existing mainframe operations introduces dependencies that can affect overall system stability.

Strategies for Stability

- **Load Balancing:**
    - Use load balancers to distribute traffic evenly across multiple servers or processing units, preventing bottlenecks and overloading.
    - Implement auto-scaling policies to add or remove resources based on real-time traffic analysis.
- **Proactive Monitoring:**

  - Deploy monitoring tools like Prometheus, Splunk, or Grafana to track system performance metrics such as latency, throughput, and error rates.
  - Set up automated alerts for anomalies, ensuring immediate response to potential issues.
- **Redundancy and Failover Mechanisms:**
  - Introduce redundant systems and failover protocols to ensure that critical operations continue uninterrupted during hardware or software failures.
  - Use distributed architectures to replicate data and processes across multiple locations for added reliability.
- **Stress Testing:**
  - Regularly perform stress tests to evaluate how the system handles peak loads and edge cases.
  - Simulate traffic spikes and component failures to identify weaknesses in the infrastructure.

---

3. Aligning Resource Planning with Organizational Goals

Why Alignment Matters

Resource allocation decisions must align with the organization's broader goals to ensure that AI/ML investments support long-term business strategies.

Steps to Align Resource Planning

- **Identify Business Priorities:**
  - Determine key objectives such as cost reduction, improved customer experiences, or enhanced

operational efficiency.
  - Ensure AI/ML resources are directed toward initiatives that drive these priorities.
- **Create a Resource Roadmap:**
  - Develop a roadmap that outlines current and future resource requirements, factoring in projected growth, new use cases, and technological advancements.
  - Align this roadmap with the organization's IT and data strategies.
- **Cost-Benefit Analysis:**
  - Evaluate the cost implications of scaling resources and compare them against expected business outcomes. For example, the savings generated by predictive maintenance may justify the investment in high-performance computing resources.
- **Collaborative Planning:**
  - Engage stakeholders across IT, data science, and business units to ensure resource planning meets diverse needs while staying within budget constraints.

Conclusion

Effective management of computational and storage resources, coupled with strategies to maintain system stability, is critical for scaling AI/ML solutions successfully. By leveraging hybrid environments, proactive monitoring, and aligned resource planning, organizations can ensure their AI/ML systems deliver consistent performance and value at scale.

In the next section, **Automating Workflows with AI/ML**, we'll explore how to use AI/ML to streamline operations, reduce manual effort, and enhance decision-making across enterprise systems.

22. Automating Workflows with AI/ML

Automation is one of the most transformative applications of AI/ML in modern enterprises. By leveraging the ability of AI/ML to learn, predict, and adapt, organizations can streamline workflows, reduce manual effort, and improve efficiency across various operations. For mainframe environments, automation offers a unique opportunity to enhance productivity and reliability while addressing the complexities of legacy systems.

In this chapter, we'll explore the potential of AI/ML-driven automation and how it can revolutionize workflows in mainframe operations.

What You'll Learn

1. Examples of Automated Processes Enabled by AI/ML

AI/ML can automate a wide range of processes, from routine tasks to complex decision-making. We'll discuss:

- How AI/ML algorithms automate processes like job scheduling, anomaly detection, and resource allocation.
- Real-world examples of automation in industries such as finance, healthcare, and logistics.
- The benefits of automation, including reduced operational costs, faster turnaround times, and improved accuracy.

2. Tools for Integrating Automation into Mainframe Operations

The integration of AI/ML-powered automation into mainframe environments requires robust tools and frameworks. We'll cover:

- Platforms and software that support AI-driven automation, such as RPA (Robotic Process Automation) tools, orchestration systems, and APIs.
- Best practices for selecting tools based on your organization's infrastructure, goals, and operational requirements.
- Strategies to ensure seamless integration and long-term scalability.

Why This Chapter Matters

AI/ML-powered automation is not just about replacing manual tasks—it's about unlocking new efficiencies and creating opportunities for innovation. By understanding the processes and tools that enable automation, organizations can elevate their mainframe operations to meet the demands of a rapidly evolving business landscape.

In the next section, **Examples of Automated Processes Enabled by AI/ML**, we'll dive into specific workflows that AI/ML can optimize, providing practical insights and inspiration for your organization.

Examples of Automated Processes Enabled by AI/ML

AI/ML-driven automation is revolutionizing workflows across industries, offering unprecedented efficiency, accuracy, and scalability. Mainframes, as the backbone of enterprise systems, are uniquely positioned to benefit from these advancements, leveraging AI/ML to automate tasks ranging from the mundane to the highly complex.

1. AI/ML-Driven Workflow Automation

Job Scheduling

AI/ML algorithms can predict resource requirements and optimize job scheduling to minimize conflicts and maximize throughput.

- **How It Works:** Machine learning models analyze historical job data to predict peak loads, enabling dynamic scheduling that avoids resource contention.
- **Example:** A financial institution's batch processing jobs are prioritized based on predicted execution times and dependencies, ensuring timely report generation.

Anomaly Detection

AI/ML models monitor system logs and transactional data in real-time, flagging irregularities that could indicate potential issues or threats.

- **How It Works:** Algorithms learn normal patterns of

system behavior and identify deviations that warrant investigation.

- **Example:** In a retail environment, AI detects unusual spikes in transaction volume, potentially indicating a security breach or system malfunction.

Resource Allocation

AI/ML enables intelligent resource allocation by predicting demand and adjusting resource distribution accordingly.

- **How It Works:** Predictive analytics assess workload trends and allocate computing resources to prevent bottlenecks and ensure high performance.
- **Example:** A healthcare system dynamically allocates storage and compute resources for electronic health records (EHR) during peak usage periods.

---

2. Real-World Examples of Automation by Industry

Finance

- **Fraud Detection:** AI models automate the monitoring of financial transactions, identifying potentially fraudulent activities in real-time.
- **Portfolio Optimization:** Machine learning algorithms analyze market trends and automate portfolio rebalancing to optimize returns.

Healthcare

- **Patient Scheduling:** AI-powered automation predicts

appointment durations and optimizes scheduling to minimize patient wait times and maximize resource utilization.

- **Diagnostic Support:** AI models analyze medical images and patient data, automating the identification of potential diagnoses for further review.

Logistics

- **Route Optimization:** AI-driven systems automate delivery route planning, reducing fuel consumption and delivery times.
- **Inventory Management:** Machine learning algorithms forecast demand and automate inventory replenishment to prevent overstocking or stockouts.

---

3. Benefits of AI/ML Automation

Reduced Operational Costs

Automation eliminates the need for manual intervention in repetitive tasks, reducing labor costs and freeing up resources for higher-value activities.

Faster Turnaround Times

AI/ML models process vast amounts of data in real-time, enabling quicker decision-making and streamlined operations.

Improved Accuracy

Machine learning algorithms learn from historical data, reducing the likelihood of errors and improving the precision of automated workflows.

Conclusion

From enhancing operational efficiency to reducing costs, AI/ML-driven automation is a transformative force for organizations leveraging mainframe systems. By automating critical workflows like job scheduling, anomaly detection, and resource allocation, enterprises can unlock new levels of productivity and reliability.

In the next section, **Tools for Integrating Automation into Mainframe Operations**, we'll explore the platforms and strategies that enable seamless AI/ML automation in complex enterprise environments.

Tools for Integrating Automation into Mainframe Operations

Integrating AI/ML-powered automation into mainframe environments involves using advanced tools and frameworks that bridge the gap between legacy systems and modern technologies. These tools streamline processes, enhance operational efficiency, and enable scalability while ensuring compatibility with existing infrastructure.

1. Platforms and Software for AI-Driven Automation

Robotic Process Automation (RPA) Tools

- **Functionality:** Automate repetitive, rule-based tasks by mimicking user interactions with mainframe applications.
- **Examples:**
  - UiPath: Offers seamless integration with mainframes for data extraction, validation, and entry.
  - Automation Anywhere: Enables end-to-end process automation with built-in AI/ML capabilities.
- **Use Case:** Automating data input and retrieval processes in banking and insurance operations.

Orchestration Systems

- **Functionality:** Manage and coordinate complex workflows across multiple systems, ensuring tasks are executed in sequence or parallel as needed.

- **Examples:**
    - Apache Airflow: Used for scheduling and monitoring workflows, with flexibility to integrate AI/ML tasks.
    - IBM Workload Automation: Tailored for mainframe environments, offering advanced scheduling and optimization.
- **Use Case:** Coordinating batch processing jobs in retail to update inventory systems and generate sales reports.

Application Programming Interfaces (APIs)

- **Functionality:** Facilitate communication between mainframes and AI/ML platforms, enabling data exchange and process automation.
- **Examples:**
    - REST APIs: For integrating modern applications with legacy systems.
    - GraphQL APIs: To optimize data retrieval and streamline queries for AI/ML models.
- **Use Case:** Real-time anomaly detection by feeding transactional data from mainframes to AI/ML systems via APIs.

---

2. Best Practices for Selecting Tools

Assess Compatibility with Mainframes

- Ensure the tools can handle mainframe-specific data formats (e.g., EBCDIC, VSAM).
- Verify support for existing mainframe operating systems such as z/OS or IBM i.

Focus on Scalability

- Choose tools that can scale with increasing data volumes and computational demands.
- Opt for platforms with cloud-native capabilities to leverage hybrid cloud environments.

Evaluate Ease of Integration

- Prioritize tools with pre-built connectors for mainframes, minimizing development effort.
- Look for solutions that offer extensive documentation and vendor support.

Align with Organizational Goals

- Select tools that address specific pain points, such as improving job scheduling, enhancing data accuracy, or enabling real-time decision-making.
- Consider tools that align with long-term automation and AI/ML strategies.

---

3. Strategies for Seamless Integration and Long-Term Scalability

Phased Rollout

- Begin with small-scale implementations to validate tool compatibility and performance.
- Gradually expand to enterprise-wide deployment, ensuring minimal disruption.

Hybrid Environment Optimization

- Use tools that support hybrid architectures, enabling data and workload distribution between mainframes and cloud systems.
- Leverage cloud resources for compute-intensive AI/ML tasks while retaining critical data on secure mainframe systems.

Continuous Monitoring and Feedback

- Implement monitoring tools to track the performance and reliability of integrated workflows.
- Regularly collect feedback from users and stakeholders to refine and enhance the automation process.

Future-Proofing

- Choose tools that are flexible and adaptable to evolving technologies, ensuring they remain relevant as AI/ML capabilities advance.
- Partner with vendors offering regular updates and enhancements.

Conclusion

Integrating AI/ML automation into mainframe operations requires robust tools and a strategic approach. By leveraging RPA platforms, orchestration systems, and APIs, organizations can automate complex workflows while maintaining compatibility with legacy systems. Adopting best practices and scalable strategies ensures these integrations deliver long-term value.

23. Best Practices for Deployment

The deployment phase is one of the most critical steps in integrating AI/ML solutions into mainframe environments. Proper execution during this phase ensures that the models and systems operate seamlessly, delivering the intended value without disrupting ongoing operations. Deployment requires meticulous planning, robust execution, and proactive monitoring to minimize risks and maintain system integrity.

In this chapter, we'll explore the essential best practices for deploying AI/ML solutions effectively in enterprise settings.

What You'll Learn

1. Minimizing Downtime and Disruption

Deployment often involves changes to mission-critical systems, making it essential to minimize interruptions. We'll discuss:

- Techniques for phased deployment, including A/B testing and canary releases, to mitigate risks.
- Strategies for maintaining operational continuity during integration, ensuring minimal impact on end users.
- The role of redundancy and failover mechanisms in safeguarding system availability.

2. Ensuring Continuous Monitoring and System Stability

Post-deployment monitoring is crucial for detecting issues early and maintaining optimal performance. We'll cover:

- Best practices for implementing real-time monitoring tools to track model and system performance.
- The importance of setting up automated alerts and dashboards for proactive issue resolution.
- Techniques for achieving long-term system stability, including load balancing, resource optimization, and regular updates.

Why This Chapter Matters

Deployment is where the promise of AI/ML solutions becomes a reality. By adhering to best practices, organizations can ensure a smooth transition, maintain user confidence, and maximize the return on their investment. A successful deployment lays the foundation for ongoing improvements and long-term system resilience.

In the next section, **Minimizing Downtime and Disruption**, we'll dive into specific strategies and methods to reduce deployment risks and ensure continuity in operations.

Minimizing Downtime and Disruption

Deploying AI/ML solutions into mainframe environments is a high-stakes process, as even minor disruptions can have significant operational and financial consequences. By adopting a systematic and risk-aware approach, organizations can integrate new technologies seamlessly while maintaining system stability and user trust.

1. Techniques for Phased Deployment

Phased deployment strategies are designed to minimize risks by implementing changes incrementally rather than all at once. This allows organizations to test new features or models in controlled environments before rolling them out system-wide.

A/B Testing

- **What It Is:** A/B testing involves deploying a new model or system to a subset of users or data while the existing system continues to serve the rest.
- **Benefits:** Provides a direct comparison of performance metrics (e.g., accuracy, latency) between the new and old systems, allowing issues to be identified and addressed early.
- **Example:** In a retail environment, an AI-driven recommendation engine can be tested with a small percentage of online users to measure its impact on sales without disrupting the entire user base.

Canary Releases

- **What It Is:** A canary release involves deploying the new model to a small, representative portion of the production environment.
- **Benefits:** Limits the exposure of potential issues, allowing organizations to monitor performance in real-world conditions without affecting all users.
- **Example:** A bank might deploy an AI-powered fraud detection system to transactions in one region before expanding it globally.

---

2. Strategies for Maintaining Operational Continuity

Maintaining seamless operations during deployment is critical, especially for mission-critical mainframe environments. These strategies can help ensure that disruptions are minimized:

Parallel Running

- **What It Is:** Running the old and new systems simultaneously for a period to validate the new system's performance.
- **Benefits:** Ensures that the new system produces the same or better results as the old one before full switchover.
- **Example:** A logistics company might run its existing scheduling algorithm alongside an AI-optimized version to compare efficiency metrics.

Pre-Deployment Testing

- **Simulated Workloads:** Use historical data to test the new system under conditions that closely mimic real-world usage.

- **Stress Testing:** Evaluate how the system performs under peak loads to identify potential bottlenecks.

Gradual Rollout

- Deploy changes incrementally across departments, regions, or time zones to reduce the risk of widespread disruption.
- Monitor each phase carefully before proceeding to the next.

---

3. The Role of Redundancy and Failover Mechanisms

To safeguard system availability during deployment, redundancy and failover mechanisms are essential. These tools and practices ensure that operations can continue even if issues arise during integration.

Redundancy

- **What It Is:** Maintaining backup systems or components that can take over if the primary system fails.
- **Example:** An e-commerce platform with redundant servers ensures uninterrupted service during a model deployment or system update.

Failover Mechanisms

- **What It Is:** Automatic switching to a backup system or configuration in the event of a failure.
- **Example:** A financial institution deploying an AI-driven credit scoring model might use a failover mechanism to revert to the traditional scoring system if anomalies are detected during deployment.

Rollback Capabilities

- **What It Is:** The ability to revert to the previous system version quickly if the new deployment encounters critical issues.
- **Example:** A healthcare provider deploying an AI-driven scheduling system can roll back to manual scheduling methods if unexpected errors occur.

Conclusion

By implementing phased deployment techniques, maintaining operational continuity, and leveraging redundancy and failover mechanisms, organizations can minimize downtime and disruption during AI/ML deployment. These strategies not only reduce risk but also build confidence among stakeholders and users.

In the next section, **Ensuring Continuous Monitoring and System Stability**, we'll explore how to maintain optimal performance and reliability after deployment, ensuring long-term success for your AI/ML solutions.

Ensuring Continuous Monitoring and System Stability

Post-deployment monitoring and maintenance are vital for ensuring that AI/ML solutions deliver consistent and reliable performance in mainframe environments. Effective monitoring systems allow organizations to detect and address potential issues before they impact operations, while stability measures help maintain system resilience over the long term.

1. Best Practices for Real-Time Monitoring

Real-time monitoring tools are essential for keeping track of both the AI/ML models and the broader system's performance. These tools provide immediate feedback and actionable insights.

Monitoring Model Performance

- **Track Metrics:** Continuously monitor key metrics like accuracy, latency, and throughput to ensure models perform as expected.
- **Drift Detection:** Use tools to identify data or concept drift, which can degrade model accuracy over time.
- **Example:** A predictive maintenance model can be monitored to ensure it continues to accurately forecast equipment failures based on evolving usage patterns.

Monitoring System Health

- **Resource Usage:** Monitor CPU, memory, and storage utilization to prevent resource bottlenecks.

- **Error Rates:** Keep track of error logs and exceptions to identify and address anomalies quickly.
- **Example:** A retail organization running a recommendation engine monitors system health to ensure that spikes in website traffic don't disrupt performance.

---

2. Automated Alerts and Dashboards

Proactive monitoring is enhanced by automation, which reduces the manual effort required to track and manage system performance.

Automated Alerts

- **Threshold-Based Alerts:** Configure alerts to notify administrators when metrics deviate from acceptable ranges.
- **Anomaly Detection Alerts:** Use AI/ML to detect patterns that indicate potential issues before they escalate.
- **Example:** An automated alert system notifies a banking institution of unusual latency in its fraud detection model, allowing quick investigation and resolution.

Dashboards

- **Centralized Insights:** Dashboards consolidate performance data, making it easy to identify trends and areas of concern.
- **Customizable Views:** Tailor dashboards to show the most relevant metrics for different stakeholders, such as IT teams, data scientists, or business leaders.
- **Example:** A logistics company uses a real-time dashboard to track the performance of its AI-driven scheduling

system, ensuring on-time deliveries.

---

3. Techniques for Long-Term System Stability

Long-term stability ensures that AI/ML solutions remain reliable and efficient as organizational needs and workloads evolve.

Load Balancing

- **Dynamic Distribution:** Use load balancers to distribute tasks and requests across multiple servers or systems evenly.
- **Example:** An e-commerce platform deploys load balancing to handle surges in traffic during holiday sales while maintaining consistent response times.

Resource Optimization

- **Scaling:** Leverage hybrid cloud environments to scale computational resources up or down based on demand.
- **Efficiency Improvements:** Optimize resource allocation by analyzing usage patterns and adjusting configurations.
- **Example:** A healthcare provider adjusts its AI-driven patient scheduling system to prioritize critical appointments during peak hours.

Regular Updates

- **Model Updates:** Retrain AI/ML models periodically with fresh data to maintain accuracy and relevance.
- **System Patches:** Apply regular updates to software, middleware, and hardware to address vulnerabilities and improve performance.

- **Example:** A financial institution updates its AI fraud detection model to incorporate new fraud patterns identified in recent transactions.

Conclusion

Continuous monitoring and proactive stability measures are essential for ensuring the success of AI/ML deployments. By using real-time monitoring tools, automated alerts, and techniques like load balancing and resource optimization, organizations can maintain the reliability and efficiency of their systems while adapting to changing needs.

Part VIII: Continuous Improvement

The integration of AI/ML into mainframe environments is not a one-time endeavor but a continuous journey. Once deployed, systems must be monitored, refined, and adapted to changing business needs and technological advancements. This final part of the book focuses on strategies to sustain and enhance the performance of AI/ML-integrated systems, ensuring their long-term value.

What This Part Covers

This section delves into the processes and practices that enable organizations to maximize the potential of their AI/ML initiatives while staying ahead in a rapidly evolving technological landscape.

1. Monitoring and Maintenance

Ongoing monitoring is essential for identifying performance issues, tracking model accuracy, and ensuring system stability. Proactive maintenance ensures that systems remain reliable and meet operational demands.

2. Retraining and Adaptation

As business requirements and data patterns change, AI/ML models must be retrained and updated to maintain their effectiveness. This part explores when and how to retrain models and avoid challenges like model drift.

3. Continuous Optimization

Optimization is about seeking incremental improvements to enhance system performance, reduce costs, and deliver better outcomes. This includes leveraging advancements in AI/ML technologies and refining workflows.

4. Looking to the Future

AI/ML integration is part of a broader transformation in mainframe environments. We'll examine emerging trends and prepare organizations for the next wave of innovation, ensuring they remain competitive and adaptable.

Why Continuous Improvement Matters

Continuous improvement ensures that your AI/ML initiatives remain aligned with business goals, scalable for growth, and resilient in the face of challenges. By fostering a culture of ongoing refinement, organizations can unlock the full potential of their investments and maintain a leadership position in their industries.

In the next section, **Monitoring AI/ML-Integrated Systems**, we'll explore how to set up robust monitoring frameworks that ensure systems perform at their best over time.

24. Monitoring AI/ML-Integrated Systems

Once AI/ML solutions are deployed, continuous monitoring becomes a critical step in ensuring they operate effectively and deliver consistent value. Monitoring enables organizations to detect potential issues, maintain performance, and make informed decisions about system improvements.

This section explores the essential tools and practices for keeping AI/ML-integrated systems running smoothly and aligned with organizational goals.

What You'll Learn

1. Tools for Real-Time Performance Tracking

AI/ML systems generate vast amounts of data, making real-time tracking essential for assessing performance and identifying areas of concern. We'll cover:

- The types of tools available for monitoring model and system metrics, including latency, accuracy, and throughput.
- Integration options for these tools within mainframe environments and hybrid architectures.
- Real-world examples of how organizations leverage performance tracking to ensure operational efficiency.

2. Setting Up Alerts and Dashboards

Monitoring becomes actionable when paired with tools that deliver timely insights and notifications. This subtopic will focus on:

- Configuring automated alerts for anomalies or deviations from expected performance.
- Designing dashboards that consolidate and visualize critical metrics in a user-friendly format.
- Best practices for ensuring that alerts and dashboards are tailored to specific business and technical needs.

Why This Matters

Effective monitoring not only ensures the reliability of AI/ML systems but also provides the foundation for continuous improvement. By implementing robust monitoring practices, organizations can proactively address issues, optimize resource utilization, and build confidence in their AI/ML initiatives.

In the next section, **Tools for Real-Time Performance Tracking**, we'll dive deeper into the technologies and strategies that make monitoring AI/ML-integrated systems efficient and effective.

Tools for Real-Time Performance Tracking

Real-time performance tracking is a cornerstone of successful AI/ML integration. By monitoring key metrics such as latency, accuracy, and throughput, organizations can ensure their systems deliver reliable and efficient results. This proactive approach helps identify potential issues before they escalate, enabling smoother operations and more effective decision-making.

1. Types of Tools for Monitoring Metrics

Several tools are available for tracking the performance of AI/ML models and the systems in which they operate. These tools cater to various needs, from basic monitoring to advanced analytics and visualization.

Model Monitoring Tools

- **Metrics Tracked:** Accuracy, precision, recall, F1 score, data drift, and model confidence levels.
- **Examples:**
  - **MLflow:** Tracks experiments, records metrics, and manages model deployments.
  - **WhyLabs:** Monitors data and model quality, offering alerts on data drift and anomalies.

System Monitoring Tools

- **Metrics Tracked:** Latency, resource utilization (CPU, memory, and storage), and throughput.

- **Examples:**
    - **Prometheus:** Open-source monitoring for system health, offering customizable metrics and alerts.
    - **Grafana:** Provides real-time data visualization, allowing users to create dynamic dashboards.
    - **AppDynamics:** Focuses on application performance, including transaction tracking and user experience metrics.

---

2. Integration Options for Mainframe and Hybrid Environments

Mainframe systems have unique requirements for integrating real-time monitoring tools, especially in hybrid architectures that combine legacy systems with cloud environments.

Mainframe-Specific Integration

- **Custom Adapters:** Tools like Splunk or Elastic Stack can be configured to ingest mainframe logs and metrics for centralized monitoring.
- **Vendor-Specific Solutions:** IBM OMEGAMON provides performance tracking for IBM Z mainframes, offering detailed insights into transaction processing and resource utilization.

Hybrid Cloud Integration

- **Cloud-Native Tools:** Platforms such as AWS CloudWatch, Azure Monitor, or Google Stackdriver offer robust monitoring for hybrid architectures. These tools can track workloads running across mainframe and cloud environments.
- **Data Pipelines:** ETL (Extract, Transform, Load) tools can

be used to route mainframe data into modern analytics platforms for real-time processing and visualization.

---

3. Real-World Examples of Performance Tracking

Example 1: Financial Services

A large bank uses Prometheus and Grafana to monitor an AI-powered fraud detection model deployed in a hybrid environment. Metrics such as response time, transaction throughput, and model confidence are tracked to ensure compliance with regulatory requirements.

Example 2: Retail Industry

An e-commerce company integrates AppDynamics to monitor the performance of its AI-driven recommendation engine. Metrics like latency during peak shopping hours and resource utilization are visualized in real-time dashboards, enabling quick optimization.

Example 3: Healthcare

A hospital uses WhyLabs to monitor its AI-based patient scheduling system. Alerts are configured to notify administrators of data drift, ensuring that model predictions remain accurate as patient demographics evolve.

Conclusion

The right tools for real-time performance tracking not only provide visibility into the health of AI/ML systems but also empower organizations to take timely, data-driven actions. By leveraging these tools and tailoring them to their unique mainframe or hybrid environments, enterprises can achieve operational excellence and unlock the full potential of AI/ML.

In the next section, **Setting Up Alerts and Dashboards**, we'll explore how to make monitoring actionable by configuring automated notifications and designing intuitive data visualizations.

Setting Up Alerts and Dashboards

Monitoring the performance of AI/ML-integrated systems is only effective if insights are actionable. Automated alerts and well-designed dashboards bridge the gap between monitoring data and operational decision-making. They enable teams to respond swiftly to anomalies, optimize performance, and maintain system reliability.

1. Configuring Automated Alerts

Alerts are a critical component of any monitoring framework, providing immediate notifications about system issues or deviations from expected behavior.

Steps for Effective Alert Configuration

- **Define Thresholds:** Establish baseline performance metrics for critical parameters such as latency, accuracy, and resource usage. For example:
    - Set a threshold for latency exceeding 500ms in a transaction processing system.
    - Trigger an alert if model accuracy drops below 90%.
- **Set Severity Levels:** Categorize alerts by priority (e.g., critical, warning, informational) to ensure appropriate escalation.
- **Implement Anomaly Detection:** Use AI/ML-based monitoring tools to detect deviations that might not meet predefined thresholds but still indicate potential issues, such as subtle data drift.

Notification Channels

- **Email and SMS:** Send immediate notifications to relevant stakeholders for critical issues.
- **Integration with Collaboration Tools:** Use platforms like Slack or Microsoft Teams for seamless communication and collaboration during incident resolution.
- **Dashboard Alerts:** Highlight alerts directly within dashboards for a comprehensive overview.

Example: Real-Time Fraud Detection

A bank configures alerts for its AI-driven fraud detection model. Anomalies such as a sudden spike in high-value transactions outside business hours trigger notifications to the fraud prevention team.

2. Designing Dashboards

Dashboards consolidate and visualize data in an intuitive format, making it easier to monitor system performance and identify trends at a glance.

Key Features of Effective Dashboards

- **Customizable Views:** Allow users to tailor dashboards based on their role or focus. For example:
  - IT teams might prioritize system health metrics.
  - Business leaders may focus on model ROI and customer impact.
- **Real-Time Updates:** Ensure dashboards display live data for immediate decision-making.
- **Visualization Tools:** Use graphs, heatmaps, and gauges to represent data in a visually engaging and comprehensible manner.

Essential Metrics to Include

- **Model Performance Metrics:** Accuracy, precision, recall, F1 score, and latency.
- **System Health Metrics:** CPU and memory utilization, throughput, and error rates.
- **Operational Insights:** Number of transactions processed, anomalies detected, or alerts triggered over a specified period.

Example: Retail Recommendation Engine

An e-commerce company creates a dashboard for its AI-based recommendation engine. It features:

- Real-time latency metrics during peak shopping hours.
- Visualizations of click-through rates for personalized recommendations.
- Heatmaps showing customer interaction patterns.

---

3. Best Practices for Tailoring Alerts and Dashboards

To maximize their impact, alerts and dashboards should be customized to align with the specific requirements of the organization.

Tailoring Alerts

- **Avoid Alert Fatigue:** Focus on critical alerts to prevent overwhelming teams with excessive notifications.
- **Actionable Notifications:** Ensure alerts provide enough context and suggested actions for efficient issue resolution.

Customizing Dashboards

- **Role-Specific Data:** Create separate dashboards for IT teams, data scientists, and business leaders to highlight the most relevant information.
- **Historical Data Comparison:** Include the ability to compare current metrics with historical trends to identify performance changes over time.
- **Interactive Features:** Allow users to drill down into specific data points for detailed analysis.

Conclusion

Setting up automated alerts and user-friendly dashboards turns monitoring data into actionable insights. Alerts enable rapid responses to issues, while dashboards provide a comprehensive view of system performance. Together, they form an essential foundation for maintaining and optimizing AI/ML-integrated systems.

25. Retraining AI/ML Models

AI/ML models are not static—they require ongoing refinement to maintain their effectiveness and relevance. Retraining ensures that models adapt to new data, evolving business needs, and changing conditions in the operational environment. Without this process, models risk becoming outdated and delivering suboptimal results.

In this section, we'll explore the key aspects of retraining AI/ML models, focusing on when to initiate retraining and how to avoid common pitfalls.

What You'll Learn

1. When and How to Retrain Models

AI/ML models must be retrained at appropriate intervals to remain aligned with their intended goals. We'll discuss:

- **Signs it's time to retrain:** Including declining performance metrics, changes in input data, or shifts in business objectives.
- **Retraining workflows:** The step-by-step process for collecting new data, updating models, and validating results.

2. Avoiding Model Drift and Maintaining Accuracy

Over time, models may experience **model drift**, where their performance deteriorates due to changes in data patterns. We'll cover:

- **Detecting model drift:** Tools and techniques for identifying when a model's predictions are no longer accurate.
- **Strategies to maintain accuracy:** Including incorporating feedback loops, expanding training datasets, and monitoring long-term performance.

Why Retraining is Essential

Without regular retraining, AI/ML models risk becoming ineffective, leading to poor decision-making and wasted resources. By understanding the principles and best practices for retraining, organizations can ensure that their AI/ML systems remain robust, accurate, and aligned with business goals.

In the next section, **When and How to Retrain Models**, we'll dive into the specific triggers and steps involved in the retraining process.

When and How to Retrain Models

Retraining is a critical process in the lifecycle of AI/ML models. It ensures models continue to provide accurate and relevant insights as new data becomes available or operational conditions evolve. This section focuses on identifying when retraining is necessary and outlining a structured workflow for effective model updates.

1. Signs It's Time to Retrain

AI/ML models are trained on historical data, but as time progresses, the real-world environment in which they operate can change. Recognizing the signs that a model requires retraining is essential to maintain its accuracy and utility.

Key Indicators for Retraining

1. **Declining Performance Metrics**
    - When a model's accuracy, precision, recall, or other key performance indicators (KPIs) drop below acceptable thresholds.
    - Example: A fraud detection model starts flagging an unusually high number of false positives due to new fraud patterns.
2. **Changes in Input Data**
    - If the characteristics of incoming data differ significantly from the training data, the model may struggle to make accurate predictions.
    - Example: A customer recommendation model trained on historical shopping patterns may need

retraining if new product categories are introduced.

3. **Shifts in Business Objectives**
    - When the goals or requirements of the organization evolve, the model must be updated to align with these changes.
    - Example: A predictive maintenance model initially focused on reducing downtime may need to shift its focus to cost optimization.
4. **Regulatory or Compliance Updates**
    - Changes in legal or industry standards may require models to incorporate new datasets or follow updated workflows.

---

2. Retraining Workflows

Retraining an AI/ML model is a systematic process that ensures the updated model performs better while maintaining compatibility with operational systems.

Step 1: Collect and Analyze New Data

- Gather fresh data from the operational environment, ensuring it reflects current patterns and trends.
- Preprocess and clean the data to maintain quality and remove inconsistencies.

Step 2: Update the Model

- **Re-train from scratch:** In some cases, the entire model is retrained using a combination of old and new data to maintain historical context.
- **Incremental training:** When computational resources or

time are limited, update the model incrementally with only the new data.

Step 3: Validate the Updated Model

- Split the data into training and testing sets to evaluate the new model's performance.
- Use cross-validation techniques to ensure robustness across different subsets of data.

Step 4: Compare and Benchmark

- Measure the updated model against the current production model to ensure it performs better or meets new objectives.
- Use KPIs such as accuracy, latency, or F1 score for comparison.

Step 5: Deploy and Monitor

- Implement the updated model in a controlled environment, such as a canary release or A/B test, before full-scale deployment.
- Continuously monitor the model post-deployment to identify any immediate issues or drift.

Practical Example: Retraining a Fraud Detection Model

1. **Sign of Retraining Need:** A financial institution notices its fraud detection model is flagging many false positives due to changing fraud patterns.
2. **Workflow Execution:**
    - Collect recent transaction data, including known fraud cases.

- Retrain the model using this new dataset while incorporating historical fraud patterns.
- Validate the updated model to ensure it reduces false positives while maintaining high recall.
- Deploy the new model in a staged rollout to assess its impact before full implementation.

Conclusion

Retraining AI/ML models is a recurring requirement to keep them aligned with evolving data, objectives, and environments. By understanding the signs that retraining is necessary and following a structured workflow, organizations can maintain high-performing models that continue to deliver value.

In the next section, **Avoiding Model Drift and Maintaining Accuracy**, we'll explore strategies to prevent performance degradation over time and ensure long-term model reliability.

Avoiding Model Drift and Maintaining Accuracy

Model drift is a common challenge in AI/ML systems. It occurs when a model's performance declines over time due to changes in the underlying data distribution or the environment it operates in. Addressing model drift proactively is critical to ensuring that the model remains effective and aligned with business objectives.

1. Detecting Model Drift

Model drift can manifest in two main forms:

- **Concept Drift:** The relationship between input data and the target variable changes. For example, customer behavior patterns evolve, affecting prediction accuracy.
- **Data Drift:** The statistical properties of the input data shift over time, even if the relationship with the target variable remains the same.

Tools and Techniques for Drift Detection

1. **Performance Monitoring**
   - Regularly track key performance metrics such as accuracy, precision, recall, or F1 score.
   - Sudden declines or gradual trends in these metrics may indicate drift.
2. **Statistical Tests**
   - Use techniques like Kolmogorov-Smirnov (KS) test or Chi-Square test to compare the

distribution of new data with the training data.
    - Significant differences suggest data drift.
3. **Model-Based Monitoring**
    - Compare model predictions against actual outcomes using a holdout dataset.
    - Increasing discrepancies indicate that the model is no longer generalizing effectively.
4. **Visualization Tools**
    - Tools like dashboards and heatmaps can help identify changes in feature importance or outlier behavior in incoming data.

Example of Drift Detection

A retail company uses an AI model for demand forecasting. Over time, it notices reduced accuracy during holiday seasons. Statistical tests reveal significant shifts in purchasing patterns, highlighting the need for retraining.

---

2. Strategies to Maintain Accuracy

Preventing or addressing model drift involves implementing strategies that keep the model adaptive and relevant.

1. Incorporating Feedback Loops

- **Continuous Learning:** Implement systems that feed new data and model outcomes back into the pipeline for ongoing retraining.
- **Example:** A fraud detection model that updates itself with confirmed fraudulent and legitimate transactions.

2. Expanding Training Datasets

- Include recent data to reflect current trends and patterns.
- Balance the dataset to account for new behaviors or scenarios that were underrepresented during initial training.

3. Regularly Monitoring Long-Term Performance

- Use automated systems to flag unusual drops in performance metrics.
- Conduct periodic audits to ensure that the model aligns with business goals.

4. Domain-Specific Enhancements

- Update feature engineering techniques to incorporate new variables or relationships identified in the data.
- Example: Adding weather data to a demand forecasting model for products sensitive to seasonal changes.

Practical Example: Maintaining a Credit Scoring Model

1. **Detection:** A credit scoring model shows declining precision in predicting defaults, prompting an investigation.
2. **Response:**
    - Conduct statistical tests to identify shifts in applicant demographics and financial behaviors.
    - Retrain the model with updated data, including new features like post-pandemic financial patterns.
    - Set up automated monitoring to track performance metrics in real time.

Conclusion

Model drift is inevitable, but its impact can be mitigated through proactive detection and adaptation strategies. By leveraging tools to identify drift early and implementing practices like feedback loops, dataset expansion, and performance monitoring, organizations can maintain high-performing AI/ML models that continue to deliver value.

26. Continuous Optimization

AI/ML integration is not a one-time achievement but an ongoing journey. Continuous optimization ensures that your systems evolve alongside your organization's needs and the rapidly advancing technological landscape. This process involves not only refining existing models and workflows but also seeking new opportunities to drive greater efficiency, accuracy, and value.

In this section, we'll explore the dual aspects of continuous optimization:

What You'll Learn

1. Identifying Opportunities for Further Improvement

AI/ML solutions should deliver measurable benefits, but there is always room to enhance their performance and expand their applications. We'll discuss:

- How to assess current workflows and identify bottlenecks or inefficiencies that AI/ML can address.
- Techniques for evaluating emerging opportunities based on cost-benefit analysis and feasibility.
- Real-world examples of iterative improvements that drive significant returns on investment.

2. Staying Updated on AI/ML and Mainframe Technologies

The AI/ML and mainframe technology landscapes are constantly evolving. Staying informed about advancements is critical to maintaining a competitive edge. We'll cover:

- Resources for tracking industry trends, tools, and frameworks that enhance AI/ML integration.
- Strategies for fostering a culture of innovation within your organization.
- Examples of cutting-edge developments that could shape the future of AI/ML in mainframe environments.

Why Continuous Optimization Matters

The competitive advantages offered by AI/ML hinge on a commitment to ongoing refinement. By actively seeking improvements and staying current with technological advances, your organization can maximize its investment in AI/ML integration while future-proofing its operations.

In the next section, **Identifying Opportunities for Further Improvement**, we'll delve into practical methods for uncovering new ways to enhance AI/ML workflows and systems.

Identifying Opportunities for Further Improvement

Continuous improvement is at the heart of maximizing the potential of AI/ML systems. Even after deployment, there are countless ways to refine processes, expand applications, and unlock greater value. Identifying these opportunities requires an analytical mindset and a structured approach.

1. Assessing Current Workflows and Identifying Bottlenecks

Analyzing Workflow Efficiency

- **Evaluate Performance Metrics:** Regularly monitor key performance indicators (KPIs) to identify areas where AI/ML models are underperforming.
    - Example: A predictive maintenance system might be missing subtle failure patterns due to incomplete feature sets.
- **Map Existing Processes:** Create a detailed workflow map to pinpoint bottlenecks or redundant steps.
    - Example: A manual step in fraud detection could be automated to accelerate response times.

Common Bottlenecks in AI/ML Workflows

- **Data Pipeline Inefficiencies:**
    - Issues like delays in data extraction or transformation can hinder real-time insights.
- **Model Latency:**
    - High response times might reduce the practicality

of models in dynamic scenarios, such as stock trading or supply chain logistics.

- **Limited Integration:**
    - AI/ML applications that operate in silos might miss the bigger picture, such as combining customer data with operational insights for cross-departmental improvements.

Identifying Gaps

- **Cross-Department Feedback:** Gather input from stakeholders across the organization to understand where AI/ML could provide additional value.
    - Example: Marketing teams may request AI-driven customer segmentation insights that the current model doesn't support.

---

2. Evaluating Emerging Opportunities

Cost-Benefit Analysis

- **Assess ROI Potential:** Compare the expected value of new AI/ML applications against their implementation costs.
    - Example: A customer churn prediction model could save significant marketing expenses by targeting retention efforts more effectively.
- **Estimate Operational Impact:** Determine how proposed improvements will influence efficiency, accuracy, or customer satisfaction.

Feasibility Considerations

- **Technical Feasibility:** Evaluate whether the organization has the necessary infrastructure, data, and expertise to implement the improvement.
- **Scalability:** Ensure that new applications can handle increased data volumes or user demands as the system evolves.

Prioritization Framework

- Rank opportunities based on their impact-to-effort ratio:
    1. **High Impact, Low Effort:** Quick wins that deliver immediate value.
    2. **High Impact, High Effort:** Long-term projects with transformative potential.
    3. **Low Impact, Low Effort:** Incremental changes that enhance efficiency.
    4. **Low Impact, High Effort:** Opportunities to deprioritize unless strategic benefits justify the investment.

---

3. Real-World Examples of Iterative Improvements

Use Case 1: Enhanced Fraud Detection

- **Initial Deployment:** A financial institution uses a fraud detection model to monitor credit card transactions.
- **Improvement Opportunity:** Analysts identify a gap in detecting new fraud patterns involving international transactions.
- **Solution:** The model is retrained with additional datasets incorporating cross-border transaction behaviors, improving its recall rate by 15%.

Use Case 2: Optimized Resource Allocation

- **Initial Deployment:** A retail company uses AI/ML to manage inventory replenishment.
- **Improvement Opportunity:** The system doesn't account for promotional events that create temporary spikes in demand.
- **Solution:** New features related to event calendars are added to the model, reducing stockouts during peak sales by 20%.

Use Case 3: Customer Personalization

- **Initial Deployment:** A streaming service recommends content based on users' viewing histories.
- **Improvement Opportunity:** Feedback indicates the recommendations lack diversity.
- **Solution:** A diversity-promoting algorithm is introduced, increasing user engagement metrics by 10%.

Conclusion

Identifying opportunities for further improvement is an iterative process that involves assessing current workflows, evaluating emerging opportunities, and learning from real-world examples. By adopting a structured approach, organizations can continuously refine their AI/ML systems to deliver sustained value and remain competitive.

In the next section, **Staying Updated on AI/ML and Mainframe Technologies**, we'll explore how to stay ahead of technological advancements and leverage them for continuous innovation.

Staying Updated on AI/ML and Mainframe Technologies

In the rapidly evolving fields of AI/ML and mainframe technology, staying informed about new tools, techniques, and trends is essential to maintaining a competitive advantage. Organizations that prioritize continuous learning and adaptation are better positioned to harness the full potential of these technologies.

1. Resources for Tracking Industry Trends and Tools

Key Information Channels

- **Industry Blogs and Publications:**
  - Websites like *Towards Data Science, KDnuggets,* and *TechTarget's SearchDataCenter* provide insights into the latest advancements in AI/ML and mainframe technology.
- **Research Papers and White Papers:**
  - Platforms like *arXiv* and *IEEE Xplore* publish cutting-edge research, offering deep dives into emerging methodologies and innovations.
- **Vendor Updates and Webinars:**
  - Follow updates from major players like IBM, AWS, Microsoft, and Google to stay informed about their new tools and services for AI/ML and mainframes.

Events and Networking Opportunities

- **Conferences and Meetups:**
  - Events such as *AI Summit, Supercomputing Conference (SC),*

and *IBM Think* offer opportunities to learn from experts and network with peers.

- **Online Communities:**
    - Engage with forums like *Reddit's r/MachineLearning, Data Science Central*, and vendor-specific communities for knowledge sharing and problem-solving.

Training and Certification Programs

- Keep skills sharp through courses and certifications from platforms like *Coursera, edX*, and vendor-specific programs (e.g., IBM Watson certifications, AWS AI/ML certifications).

---

2. Strategies for Fostering a Culture of Innovation

Encourage Lifelong Learning

- **Upskilling Employees:**
    - Provide access to training programs and workshops that cover both foundational and advanced topics in AI/ML and mainframe technologies.
- **Knowledge Sharing:**
    - Create internal forums, lunch-and-learn sessions, or hackathons to encourage collaboration and innovation.

Embrace Cross-Functional Collaboration

- AI/ML integration benefits from diverse perspectives. Encourage teams from IT, operations, and business units to collaborate on innovation projects.

Invest in Experimentation

- Establish an innovation lab or dedicate resources to pilot projects where employees can explore new technologies with minimal risk.

---

3. Examples of Cutting-Edge Developments

AI/ML Developments

- **Generative AI:**
    - Tools like GPT-based models and DALL-E are transforming content creation and problem-solving processes across industries.
- **AutoML:**
    - Automated Machine Learning platforms (e.g., Google's AutoML, H2O.ai) are simplifying model development and making AI accessible to non-experts.
- **Explainable AI (XAI):**
    - Techniques for interpreting model decisions are becoming critical, especially in regulated industries.

Mainframe Innovations

- **Quantum-Ready Algorithms:**
    - Research into quantum computing integration with mainframes is gaining momentum, with potential applications in optimization and encryption.
- **Cloud-Connected Mainframes:**

    - Hybrid cloud models are enhancing the flexibility and scalability of mainframe systems, bridging the gap between legacy systems and modern applications.

Real-World Applications

- **Predictive Healthcare Analytics:**
    - Mainframes integrated with AI/ML are helping hospitals predict patient outcomes and optimize resource allocation.
- **Real-Time Fraud Detection:**
    - Financial institutions are using AI-powered anomaly detection to flag suspicious transactions as they occur.

Conclusion

Keeping pace with advancements in AI/ML and mainframe technologies requires leveraging reliable resources, fostering a culture of continuous innovation, and staying attuned to cutting-edge developments. By doing so, organizations can remain agile, adaptive, and ready to seize new opportunities.

27. Looking Ahead: The Future of Mainframes and AI/ML

As technology continues to evolve at an unprecedented pace, the intersection of mainframes and AI/ML presents new opportunities and challenges. This chapter delves into the forward-looking aspects of these technologies, helping organizations prepare for the next wave of innovation while staying competitive.

What You'll Learn

1. Emerging Trends and Technologies to Watch

Mainframes and AI/ML are no longer standalone technologies but key enablers of broader digital transformation. We'll explore:

- **Advancements in AI/ML Algorithms:** How innovations like federated learning, generative AI, and self-supervised learning are reshaping the AI landscape.
- **Integration with Quantum Computing:** The potential impact of quantum-ready algorithms on mainframe applications.
- **The Evolution of Hybrid Systems:** The growing role of hybrid cloud architectures and edge computing in enhancing mainframe capabilities.

These emerging trends highlight the importance of adaptability and proactive planning to capitalize on future advancements.

2. Preparing for the Next Stage of Innovation

Staying ahead in the technology race requires a structured approach to innovation and transformation. We'll cover:

- **Strategic Planning for Future Technologies:** How to align business goals with upcoming advancements in AI/ML and mainframes.
- **Building an Innovation-Ready Workforce:** Equipping teams with the skills and mindset needed to embrace change.
- **Investing in Scalable Infrastructure:** Ensuring your systems are ready to support new tools, workloads, and capabilities as they emerge.

By preparing today, organizations can position themselves as leaders in tomorrow's AI/ML-driven world.

Why This Matters

The future of mainframes and AI/ML lies in their ability to adapt and evolve alongside other transformative technologies. Understanding emerging trends and planning for the next stage of innovation will empower your organization to remain resilient and forward-thinking.

In the next section, **Emerging Trends and Technologies to Watch**, we'll explore the most promising developments shaping the future of mainframes and AI/ML.

Emerging Trends and Technologies to Watch

Mainframes and AI/ML technologies are evolving in tandem with broader advancements in the tech landscape. By understanding the trends reshaping these fields, organizations can anticipate opportunities for innovation and maintain a competitive edge. Here's an in-depth look at the key emerging trends:

1. Advancements in AI/ML Algorithms

Federated Learning

Federated learning enables AI models to be trained across multiple decentralized devices or servers without sharing sensitive data. This is particularly relevant for industries like finance and healthcare, where data privacy and security are paramount.

- **Why it matters:** Mainframes, often handling sensitive data, can integrate federated learning to build smarter AI solutions while ensuring data remains local.
- **Example use case:** Fraud detection across financial institutions without exposing proprietary transaction data.

Generative AI

Generative AI, exemplified by technologies like GPT and DALL-E, allows systems to create new content based on learned patterns. This has applications ranging from content generation to complex simulation modeling.

- **Why it matters:** Mainframes can leverage generative AI to model scenarios, optimize workflows, or predict outcomes with greater precision.
- **Example use case:** Simulating demand in supply chain logistics to improve resource allocation.

Self-Supervised Learning

Self-supervised learning bridges the gap between supervised and unsupervised learning by allowing models to learn from large volumes of unlabeled data.

- **Why it matters:** Mainframes typically handle massive datasets. Self-supervised learning can unlock insights without the costly process of data labeling.
- **Example use case:** Analyzing operational logs to predict system bottlenecks or hardware failures.

---

2. Integration with Quantum Computing

Quantum-Ready Algorithms

Quantum computing is emerging as a transformative technology for solving problems beyond the scope of classical systems. Quantum-ready algorithms are designed to take advantage of this capability, particularly in optimization and cryptography.

- **Why it matters:** Mainframes, with their unmatched reliability and scalability, are natural candidates for hosting quantum-enhanced applications in hybrid setups.
- **Example use case:** Accelerating complex financial simulations or supply chain optimizations.

Future Implications

As quantum computing matures, mainframe environments integrated with quantum capabilities will redefine how enterprises approach data-intensive tasks. Investing in quantum-ready strategies today ensures preparedness for the quantum revolution.

---

3. The Evolution of Hybrid Systems

Hybrid Cloud Architectures

Hybrid cloud setups enable organizations to balance on-premises mainframe operations with the scalability and flexibility of the cloud.

- **Why it matters:** By seamlessly integrating AI/ML workloads between mainframes and cloud platforms, organizations can achieve cost-effective scalability without compromising performance or security.
- **Example use case:** Offloading AI model training to cloud resources while maintaining real-time inference on mainframe systems.

Edge Computing

Edge computing brings computation and data storage closer to the source of data generation, reducing latency and improving responsiveness.

- **Why it matters:** Coupling mainframes with edge nodes allows for distributed AI/ML processing, ideal for real-time applications in IoT or mission-critical systems.
- **Example use case:** Real-time anomaly detection in manufacturing processes using edge devices, with

mainframes handling overarching analysis.

Conclusion

These emerging trends underscore the dynamic potential of AI/ML and mainframe integration. By embracing advancements in algorithms, preparing for quantum computing, and leveraging hybrid and edge architectures, organizations can future-proof their operations and unlock unprecedented value.

In the next section, **Preparing for the Next Stage of Innovation**, we'll explore actionable strategies for adopting these trends and positioning your organization as a leader in the AI/ML-enabled future.

Preparing for the Next Stage of Innovation

As technology evolves, organizations must proactively adapt to emerging trends to remain competitive. Preparing for the next stage of innovation involves aligning strategy, workforce, and infrastructure with the transformative potential of AI/ML and mainframe technologies. Here's how organizations can approach this process effectively:

1. Strategic Planning for Future Technologies

Aligning Business Goals with Advancements

To fully harness the potential of AI/ML and mainframes, organizations must ensure their technological roadmap aligns with overarching business objectives.

- **Actionable Steps:**
  - Conduct a gap analysis to identify where current systems fall short in supporting business goals.
  - Prioritize AI/ML use cases that directly address organizational pain points, such as improving customer experiences or optimizing operations.
  - Develop a phased plan for adopting emerging technologies, ensuring a balance between innovation and risk management.

Forecasting Technology Trends

Anticipating technological shifts is essential for staying ahead of competitors.

- **Example:** Investing in hybrid cloud architectures now positions organizations to leverage quantum computing and edge AI in the future.

---

2. Building an Innovation-Ready Workforce

Equipping Teams with Relevant Skills

An organization's ability to innovate hinges on the expertise and adaptability of its workforce.

- **Skill Development Areas:**
    - **AI/ML Expertise:** Provide training on algorithm development, data science, and model deployment.
    - **Mainframe Modernization:** Equip IT teams with knowledge of APIs, middleware, and hybrid system integration.
    - **Emerging Technologies:** Offer exposure to quantum computing fundamentals, edge AI, and federated learning.

Fostering a Culture of Innovation

Innovation thrives in environments that encourage experimentation and collaboration.

- **Best Practices:**
    - Create cross-functional teams to bridge the gap between data scientists, mainframe engineers, and business leaders.
    - Reward innovation initiatives that deliver measurable outcomes, reinforcing a mindset of continuous improvement.

---

3. Investing in Scalable Infrastructure

Ensuring Readiness for Emerging Tools

Scalability is critical for integrating new tools and managing growing workloads.

- **Key Considerations:**
    - Adopt cloud-native solutions and containerization technologies to enable seamless scaling of AI/ML workloads.
    - Invest in high-performance storage and networking solutions to support data-intensive operations.

Building a Resilient Foundation

Prepare your systems to handle future demands without compromising reliability.

- **Focus Areas:**
    - Implement redundancy and disaster recovery plans to safeguard mission-critical operations.
    - Leverage hybrid architectures to distribute workloads efficiently between mainframes and cloud environments.

Conclusion

Preparing for the next stage of innovation requires a holistic approach that aligns strategic planning, workforce development, and infrastructure investment. By adopting these strategies, organizations can position themselves as leaders in the rapidly evolving landscape of AI/ML and mainframe technologies.

Part IX: Additional Resources and Next Steps

As you conclude your journey through the comprehensive exploration of AI/ML integration with mainframes, it's important to look ahead and arm yourself with additional resources that reinforce what you've learned. This final part of the companion book is designed to provide actionable insights, practical tools, and pathways for continuous growth.

AI/ML integration is not a one-time initiative but an ongoing process of innovation and refinement. Whether you're implementing solutions, scaling operations, or seeking new opportunities, the resources and strategies presented here will empower you to drive meaningful results.

What to Expect in This Section

This section offers valuable additions to your learning and implementation toolkit, focusing on three key areas:

1. Real-World Case Studies

Understanding how other organizations have successfully navigated the complexities of AI/ML and mainframe integration provides actionable inspiration. You'll explore diverse scenarios showcasing challenges, solutions, and outcomes to guide your own initiatives.

2. Tools and Technologies

A curated list of recommended tools and platforms will help you identify the right solutions for your specific needs. From cutting-edge AI/ML frameworks to mainframe-friendly integration tools, these resources will streamline your implementation efforts.

3. Lifelong Learning Opportunities

Staying ahead in this evolving landscape requires a commitment to continuous education. Discover courses, certifications, and professional networks that will keep you informed and equipped for future advancements.

Why This Matters

The insights and resources presented in this section will enable you to:

- **Learn from the best:** Adopt proven strategies from successful AI/ML implementations.
- **Equip your team:** Leverage tools and technologies to drive efficiency and innovation.
- **Stay future-ready:** Invest in ongoing education to remain at the forefront of AI/ML and mainframe advancements.

With these resources, you're not just concluding a learning journey but laying the groundwork for sustained success in AI/ML integration.

In the next section, **Case Studies and Success Stories**, we'll delve into real-world examples that illustrate the transformative potential of AI/ML in mainframe environments.

28. Case Studies and Success Stories

Learning from real-world examples is one of the most powerful ways to understand the practical applications and benefits of AI/ML integration with mainframes. Case studies and success stories offer a window into the challenges organizations have faced, the solutions they've implemented, and the measurable results they've achieved.

This section is designed to inspire and inform by showcasing how industry leaders have successfully navigated the complexities of modernization and AI/ML adoption.

What to Expect

Insights from Industry Leaders

Explore how top organizations across various industries—such as finance, healthcare, and retail—have leveraged AI/ML to enhance their mainframe operations. Each example will include:

- **Challenges faced:** A deep dive into the specific hurdles these organizations encountered, such as legacy system constraints or data quality issues.
- **Solutions implemented:** The tools, strategies, and workflows adopted to overcome these challenges.
- **Outcomes achieved:** The tangible results, including cost savings, operational efficiencies, and improved customer experiences.

Why This Matters

By studying these real-world cases, you'll gain:

- **Actionable insights:** Learn strategies that you can adapt to your organization's unique needs.
- **Proof of potential:** Understand the transformative impact AI/ML can have when applied effectively in mainframe environments.
- **Inspiration for innovation:** Identify opportunities to replicate or build upon the successes of industry leaders.

In the upcoming section, **Insights from Industry Leaders**, we'll take a closer look at these success stories, offering detailed examples that highlight the power of AI/ML integration in mainframe systems.

Insights from Industry Leaders

Top organizations across industries have demonstrated the transformative potential of integrating AI/ML into their mainframe environments. By addressing challenges, adopting innovative solutions, and achieving measurable outcomes, these industry leaders provide a roadmap for success.

Here's a closer look at how organizations in finance, healthcare, and retail have leveraged AI/ML to enhance their operations.

1. Finance: Modernizing Risk Analysis and Fraud Detection

Challenges Faced:

- Legacy systems struggling to process increasing volumes of financial transactions.
- Difficulty detecting sophisticated fraud patterns in real time.
- Maintaining regulatory compliance while modernizing operations.

Solutions Implemented:

- Deployed AI-powered fraud detection models that analyze transaction data in real time for anomalies.
- Integrated machine learning algorithms into mainframes to improve credit risk analysis, enabling dynamic updates to scoring models.
- Used hybrid cloud systems to offload intensive computations, ensuring scalability without compromising

data security.

Outcomes Achieved:

- Reduced fraud detection time from hours to minutes, preventing potential losses.
- Increased accuracy in credit risk assessments, improving lending decisions.
- Enhanced customer trust and operational efficiency by ensuring uninterrupted service.

---

2. Healthcare: Improving Patient Care with Predictive Analytics

Challenges Faced:

- Managing and analyzing vast amounts of patient data stored on legacy systems.
- Identifying at-risk patients early to prevent complications and reduce hospital readmissions.
- Ensuring data security and compliance with regulations like HIPAA.

Solutions Implemented:

- Trained machine learning models on historical patient data to predict readmission risks and recommend preventive measures.
- Deployed AI-driven natural language processing (NLP) tools to extract actionable insights from unstructured medical records.
- Integrated mainframes with cloud-based AI platforms for advanced analytics while keeping sensitive data securely on-premise.

Outcomes Achieved:

- Improved patient outcomes through early intervention and personalized care plans.
- Reduced readmission rates by over 20%, leading to significant cost savings for healthcare providers.
- Streamlined compliance processes, minimizing the risk of regulatory penalties.

---

3. Retail: Enhancing Customer Engagement with Personalization

Challenges Faced:

- Adapting to changing customer expectations for personalized experiences.
- Processing and analyzing high-velocity data from online and in-store channels.
- Scaling operations during peak shopping seasons without affecting performance.

Solutions Implemented:

- Leveraged machine learning models to analyze purchase histories and recommend personalized product offerings.
- Implemented AI-driven demand forecasting to optimize inventory management and reduce stockouts.
- Integrated mainframe systems with AI-powered chatbots to enhance customer service and reduce response times.

Outcomes Achieved:

- Increased sales and customer loyalty through personalized

recommendations and targeted promotions.

- Reduced inventory costs by optimizing stock levels based on accurate demand predictions.
- Improved customer satisfaction with faster and more efficient support.

Key Takeaways

The examples above highlight recurring themes in successful AI/ML integration:

- **Tackling challenges head-on:** These organizations embraced modernization despite the complexity of legacy systems.
- **Adopting innovative solutions:** Tailored tools and strategies enabled seamless integration of AI/ML capabilities.
- **Delivering measurable outcomes:** Tangible benefits such as cost savings, operational improvements, and enhanced customer experiences underscore the value of AI/ML.

By studying these success stories, you can identify opportunities to apply similar strategies in your own organization, driving innovation and achieving long-term growth.

29. Recommended Tools and Technologies

The successful integration of AI/ML with mainframes requires the right set of tools and technologies. From frameworks for building and training models to platforms that simplify deployment and monitoring, having the appropriate resources at your disposal is essential for ensuring efficiency and scalability.

This section provides a comprehensive guide to the tools and technologies that have proven effective in AI/ML integration within mainframe environments. Whether you're just starting or looking to optimize your existing workflows, these recommendations will help you make informed decisions tailored to your specific needs.

What to Expect

A Comprehensive List of Resources

We'll introduce a wide range of tools and technologies, categorized for ease of understanding:

- **AI/ML Frameworks:** Open-source and enterprise-grade platforms for developing and training machine learning models.
- **Data Integration Tools:** Solutions for extracting, transforming, and loading mainframe data into modern AI/ML pipelines.
- **Deployment and Monitoring Platforms:** Tools to streamline the integration of AI/ML models into mainframe systems and ensure their performance.

- **Security and Compliance Solutions:** Technologies to safeguard sensitive data and meet regulatory requirements.

Why This Matters

With the vast array of tools available, selecting the right ones can be overwhelming. By focusing on technologies that align with mainframe-specific needs, this section will:

- **Save you time:** Narrow down your options to the most relevant and effective tools.
- **Enhance productivity:** Equip you with resources that streamline development, integration, and monitoring.
- **Support scalability:** Highlight solutions that can grow alongside your AI/ML initiatives.

In the next section, **A Comprehensive List of Resources**, we'll dive deeper into each category, providing detailed descriptions, use cases, and practical tips for leveraging these tools effectively.

A Comprehensive List of Resources

Successfully integrating AI/ML into mainframe environments requires the right mix of tools and technologies to support each stage of the process. Below is an organized overview of key resources, tailored for ease of selection based on specific needs.

1. AI/ML Frameworks

These platforms form the backbone of AI/ML development, enabling model training, testing, and optimization.

Open-Source Frameworks

- **TensorFlow:** Known for its versatility and scalability, TensorFlow supports deep learning and machine learning workloads. Ideal for both beginner-friendly experimentation and enterprise-grade applications.
- **PyTorch:** A favorite for research and production, PyTorch excels in dynamic computation graphs and flexibility during experimentation.
- **Scikit-learn:** Best suited for classical machine learning tasks, Scikit-learn is lightweight and perfect for smaller, straightforward projects.

Enterprise-Grade Platforms

- **IBM Watson Studio:** Seamlessly integrates with mainframe systems and offers AI/ML capabilities tailored to industries like finance and healthcare.
- **SAS Viya:** Combines advanced analytics with machine

learning, designed for organizations managing large-scale operations on mainframes.

---

2. Data Integration Tools

Preparing mainframe data for AI/ML requires robust ETL (Extract, Transform, Load) processes and seamless data migration tools.

ETL Solutions

- **Informatica PowerCenter:** Specializes in integrating diverse data formats, including legacy mainframe formats, into unified pipelines.
- **Talend:** Offers an open-source suite for building scalable data integration workflows and handling large datasets.

Mainframe-Specific Tools

- **IBM DataStage:** A go-to tool for transforming and integrating mainframe data into modern AI/ML platforms.
- **Syncsort DMX-h:** Optimized for processing high volumes of data from mainframes to analytics environments.

---

3. Deployment and Monitoring Platforms

After models are trained, ensuring their seamless deployment and real-time performance tracking is crucial.

Deployment Tools

- **Docker:** Simplifies the packaging and deployment of AI/

ML models across different environments, including mainframes and hybrid systems.

- **Kubernetes:** Facilitates the orchestration of containerized applications for scalability and fault tolerance.

Monitoring Platforms

- **Prometheus:** An open-source system for real-time metrics monitoring, tailored to handle complex environments.
- **Splunk:** Provides actionable insights into operational performance with advanced analytics and visualization capabilities.

---

4. Security and Compliance Solutions

Ensuring data integrity and meeting regulatory standards are non-negotiable in mainframe environments.

Encryption Tools

- **Vormetric Data Security Platform:** Protects sensitive data across hybrid environments, ensuring compliance with industry regulations.
- **IBM Guardium:** Offers robust encryption, monitoring, and auditing features designed for enterprise-scale mainframe operations.

Compliance Management

- **OneTrust:** Simplifies compliance with frameworks like GDPR and HIPAA by providing tools for privacy management and data governance.

- **TrustArc:** Enables organizations to manage risk and compliance through automated workflows and reporting features.

Key Takeaways

By leveraging the right tools, organizations can:

- Streamline their AI/ML workflows, from data preparation to model deployment.
- Ensure the seamless integration of modern AI/ML capabilities into legacy mainframe systems.
- Enhance security and compliance while maintaining operational efficiency.

Each of these resources is designed to address a specific aspect of AI/ML integration, ensuring a smoother journey toward modernization and innovation.

30. Continuing Education Opportunities

The journey of integrating AI/ML with mainframes doesn't end with completing this book or a single implementation project. Staying ahead in a rapidly evolving technological landscape requires ongoing learning and skill development. Continuing education opportunities provide a pathway to deepen your expertise, explore emerging trends, and gain recognized credentials to bolster your career.

This section highlights the resources available for lifelong learning, focusing on courses and certifications tailored to AI/ML and mainframe integration.

What to Expect

1. Courses for Further Learning

We'll explore a variety of specialized courses designed to expand your knowledge in AI/ML and mainframe systems. These courses cater to various skill levels, from beginner to advanced, and cover topics like:

- Advanced AI/ML techniques for mainframe environments.
- Hybrid cloud architectures and their role in scaling AI/ML workloads.
- Tools and frameworks for mainframe modernization.

2. Certifications in AI/ML and Mainframes

Certifications validate your skills and demonstrate your expertise to employers and peers. We'll review:

- Recognized certifications from industry leaders like IBM, Google, and Microsoft.
- Mainframe-specific credentials that showcase your ability to manage legacy systems while embracing modern innovations.
- The benefits of certifications in advancing your career and staying competitive in a dynamic field.

Why It Matters

Investing in continuing education equips you with the knowledge and tools to:

- Stay updated on the latest trends and advancements in AI/ML and mainframes.
- Adapt to new challenges and technologies as they emerge.
- Enhance your professional value and career prospects in a competitive job market.

In the following sections, we'll delve deeper into these opportunities, providing guidance on selecting the right courses and certifications to support your goals.

Courses for Further Learning

Continuing education through specialized courses is essential for staying competitive in the evolving fields of AI/ML and mainframe integration. These courses not only deepen your technical expertise but also provide actionable knowledge that can be directly applied to real-world challenges.

Advanced AI/ML Techniques for Mainframe Environments

Mainframes present unique challenges and opportunities for AI/ML applications. Courses focusing on advanced techniques provide:

- **Deep Learning on Mainframes:** Explore neural networks and their applications, such as image recognition, natural language processing, and predictive modeling in a mainframe context.
- **Federated Learning for Secure Data Sharing:** Learn about distributed AI training across mainframe systems without compromising sensitive data.
- **Scalable Model Optimization:** Techniques for fine-tuning models to handle the high transaction volumes and critical workloads typical of mainframe systems.

Hybrid Cloud Architectures and Their Role in Scaling AI/ML Workloads

The integration of hybrid cloud environments with mainframes is a game-changer for scaling AI/ML solutions. Courses in this area teach:

- **Designing Hybrid Architectures:** Building efficient pipelines that balance on-premises mainframe capabilities with cloud resources for scalability and cost efficiency.
- **Cloud-Native AI Tools for Mainframes:** Leveraging platforms like AWS SageMaker, Azure Machine Learning, and Google AI Platform to enhance mainframe operations.
- **Workload Distribution Strategies:** Techniques for dynamically allocating AI/ML tasks between mainframes and cloud systems to optimize performance.

Tools and Frameworks for Mainframe Modernization

Modernizing mainframe environments is critical for unlocking the full potential of AI/ML. Courses on this topic cover:

- **Introduction to ETL and Data Transformation Tools:** Using technologies like Informatica, Talend, and IBM DataStage to prepare mainframe data for AI/ML workflows.
- **AI/ML Integration Platforms:** Hands-on training with tools like IBM Watson Studio, SAS Viya, and TensorFlow.
- **Automation and Orchestration Frameworks:** Learning to implement automation for job scheduling, anomaly detection, and other operational tasks using AI/ML tools.

Benefits of Continuing Education through Courses

- **Practical Expertise:** Gain hands-on experience with tools and techniques specific to your industry.
- **Flexibility:** Many courses are available online, making it easier to balance learning with professional commitments.

- **Targeted Learning:** Courses cater to both general AI/ML concepts and mainframe-specific challenges, allowing you to tailor your education to your needs.

By pursuing these courses, you'll gain the skills necessary to address complex challenges, implement innovative solutions, and stay at the forefront of your field.

Certifications in AI/ML and Mainframes

Certifications are a powerful way to validate your expertise, enhance your professional credibility, and demonstrate your commitment to staying at the forefront of technological advancements. Whether you're an AI/ML specialist or a mainframe professional, certifications provide structured learning paths and industry-recognized credentials that can significantly boost your career prospects.

Recognized Certifications from Industry Leaders

Leading technology companies and organizations offer certifications tailored to AI/ML and system integration. These include:

IBM Certifications

- **IBM Certified AI Practitioner:** Focuses on foundational AI skills, including machine learning and neural networks, with applications in enterprise systems.
- **IBM z/OS Mainframe Practitioner:** Provides a deep understanding of IBM mainframe environments, including tools and best practices for managing legacy systems.

Google Certifications

- **Google Professional Machine Learning Engineer:** Covers the design, implementation, and management of ML models, with an emphasis on integrating with hybrid cloud environments.

- **Google Cloud Certified – Professional Data Engineer:** Highlights skills in data pipeline management and AI integration with enterprise systems, applicable to mainframe data handling.

Microsoft Certifications

- **Microsoft Certified: Azure AI Engineer Associate:** Focuses on building and managing AI solutions using Microsoft Azure tools, including scenarios involving mainframe integration.
- **Microsoft Certified: Data Scientist Associate:** Equips learners with knowledge of AI/ML techniques and their applications in enterprise data systems.

Mainframe-Specific Credentials

Certifications that bridge the gap between traditional mainframe operations and modern innovations include:

- **CompTIA Server+ Certification:** Focuses on server and system maintenance, including the integration of AI/ML technologies into legacy infrastructures.
- **Mainframe Modernization Certifications from IBM:** Courses and credentials designed to train professionals on using AI/ML and hybrid cloud technologies in mainframe settings.

The Benefits of Certifications

Certifications are more than just badges—they are evidence of your capability to implement advanced technologies effectively. Benefits include:

Career Advancement

- Certifications make your resume stand out, particularly in competitive fields like AI/ML and mainframe modernization.
- They often lead to higher-paying roles and greater responsibilities within organizations.

Demonstrated Expertise

- Certifications validate your ability to solve real-world problems using AI/ML and mainframe systems.
- They give employers confidence in your skills and understanding of best practices.

Staying Competitive in a Dynamic Field

- The technology landscape is constantly evolving; certifications help you stay current with emerging tools and frameworks.
- They enable you to align your skills with the latest industry demands, ensuring long-term relevance.

Conclusion

By pursuing certifications in AI/ML and mainframe technologies, you position yourself as a knowledgeable and capable professional ready to tackle the challenges of today's interconnected, data-driven enterprises.

Epilogue

As we conclude this journey into the integration of Artificial Intelligence and Machine Learning with mainframe environments, it's clear that the convergence of these technologies is not just a fleeting trend but a foundational shift in enterprise operations. Mainframes, once seen as legacy systems, are proving their enduring value by adapting to modern innovations and supporting advanced AI/ML capabilities.

The tools, techniques, and strategies outlined in this book are designed to empower you to navigate this transformation with confidence. Whether you are optimizing workloads, enhancing security, or driving predictive analytics, your ability to bridge the gap between traditional systems and cutting-edge technologies positions you as a leader in your field.

A Future of Possibilities

The integration of AI/ML with mainframes opens a world of opportunities:

- **Operational Excellence:** Automating processes and improving resource allocation will redefine efficiency across industries.
- **Business Innovation:** Leveraging AI/ML for data-driven decision-making will enable organizations to uncover new growth avenues.
- **Scalable Systems:** Hybrid architectures and continuous optimization ensure that mainframes remain vital in a rapidly changing technological landscape.

These possibilities are not theoretical—they are actionable, achievable, and within your grasp.

Your Role as a Change Agent

The journey does not end here. As you implement the strategies and knowledge gained from this book, you become a catalyst for innovation within your organization. Your expertise in integrating AI/ML into mainframe environments will:

- **Inspire Confidence:** Showcasing the value of modernization to stakeholders and teams.
- **Drive Results:** Delivering measurable improvements that align with organizational goals.
- **Shape the Future:** Contributing to the evolution of enterprise technology and setting new standards for excellence.

Looking Ahead

Technology never stands still. As AI/ML and mainframe systems continue to evolve, staying informed and adaptable will be key. Keep exploring, learning, and experimenting. Seek out continuing education opportunities, engage with industry leaders, and remain open to new ideas.

This is your moment to lead in a transformative era. By embracing innovation and leveraging your skills, you are not only future-proofing mainframes but also driving a vision of progress and resilience for the enterprises of tomorrow.

Thank you for embarking on this journey. The future of mainframes and AI/ML integration is bright, and it's professionals like you who will ensure its success.

Don't miss out!

Visit the website below and you can sign up to receive emails whenever Ricardo Nuqui publishes a new book. There's no charge and no obligation.

https://books2read.com/r/B-A-NBRMC-DBQIF

BOOKS 2 READ

Connecting independent readers to independent writers.

Did you love *Future-Proof Your Mainframes with AI/ML*? Then you should read *Mainframe Containerization Mastery*[1] by Ricardo Nuqui!

[2]

Unlock the future of your organization with ***Mainframe Containerization Mastery***. This comprehensive guide is designed for IT leaders, systems managers, and technical professionals looking to modernize their mainframe applications and seamlessly integrate them into cloud-native environments.

As businesses strive for agility, scalability, and cost-effectiveness, mainframe containerization emerges as a pivotal solution. This book delves deep into the principles, technologies, and best practices of containerization, offering practical insights into transforming traditional mainframe systems into dynamic, flexible assets.

---

1. https://books2read.com/u/b5K257

2. https://books2read.com/u/b5K257

Inside, you'll discover:

A thorough exploration of containerization technology, including Docker and Kubernetes, tailored specifically for mainframe environments.Step-by-step guidance on assessing application readiness, optimizing performance, and ensuring robust security in hybrid systems.Real-world use cases showcasing successful implementations in sectors such as finance, healthcare, e-commerce, and logistics.Advanced topics that address the challenges of large enterprises, DevOps integration, and emerging trends in mainframe and cloud synergy.

Whether you're embarking on a containerization journey or seeking to refine your existing strategy, this book equips you with the knowledge and tools to navigate the complexities of hybrid IT infrastructures. Join the revolution in mainframe modernization and harness the power of containerization to drive your organization forward.

Also by Ricardo Nuqui

Mainframes

Mastering Mainframe Modernization
Mainframe Meets Modernization: Mastering Hybrid Cloud Design
Mainframe Mastery with DevOps: Integrating Legacy Systems with Agile Practices
Mainframe Modernization: CI/CD Mastery
Mainframe to Cloud Mastery: Best Practices
Mainframe Modernization with DevOps Mastery
Mainframe Containerization Mastery
Future-Proof Your Mainframes with AI/ML

www.ingramcontent.com/pod-product-compliance
Lightning Source LLC
LaVergne TN
LVHW052221200926
848481LV00001B/171
9789815194944